Reading ECPE

Eight practice tests for the revised 2021 **Michigan exam**

Fiona Aish and Jo Tomlinson

PROSPERITY EDUCATION
www.prosperityeducation.net

Registered offices: Sherlock Close, Cambridge
CB3 0HP, United Kingdom

© Prosperity Education Ltd. 2023

First published 2023

ISBN: 978-1-913825-63-8

This publication is in copyright. Subject to statutory exception and to the provisions of relevant collective licensing agreements, no reproduction of any part may take place without the written permission of Prosperity Education.

'ECPE' is a brand belonging to the University of Michigan and Cambridge Assessment English, and is not associated with Prosperity Education or its products.

The moral rights of the authors have been asserted.

For further information and resources, visit:
www.prosperityeducation.net

To infinity and beyond

Contents

Introduction	v
Test 1	1
Test 2	15
Test 3	29
Test 4	43
Test 5	57
Test 6	71
Test 7	85
Test 8	99
Answers	113

Introduction

Welcome to this edition of sample tests for the Michigan Language Assessment Examination for the Certificate of Proficiency in English (ECPE), designed specifically for students preparing for the challenging GCVR (Parts 1–4: Grammar, Cloze, Vocabulary and Reading) section of the examination.

The content has been written to closely replicate the ECPE experience, and has undergone comprehensive expert and peer review. You or your students, if you are a teacher, will hopefully enjoy the wide range of text topics and benefit from the repetitive practice, something that is key to preparing for the GCVR section of the examination.

Each test comprises 70 multiple-choice questions, each carrying one mark, and candidates are given 75 minutes in which to complete the four parts of the GCVR section:

1. Grammar: 16 questions testing grammatical fluency, phrasal verb particles, word formation and prepositions.

2. Cloze (multiple choice): 20 questions testing lexical and grammatical ability within the context of two texts, each comprising 200–250 words.

3. Vocabulary: 16 questions testing knowledge of phrasal verbs, phrases and idioms.

4. Reading: 18 questions testing candidates' understanding of meaning in context, reference words, implication, purpose and tone within the context of three texts, each comprising 300–350 words.

We hope that you will find this resource a useful study aid, and we wish you all the best in preparing for the exam.

Fiona Aish and Jo Tomlinson

Fiona Aish and Jo Tomlinson are directors of Target English, a consultancy that provides tailor-made solutions in content creation, course provision, training and testing.

Reading ECPE
Test 1

Reading ECPE

51 The generous donation was accepted _____ it did not imply any influence on the university's running.

- A in the event that
- B on the condition that
- C with admission that
- D as long as that

52 _____ the book sold more than six-million copies, it's also up for an award.

- A Not only has
- B Hardly had not
- C Far more than
- D Just barely has

53 _____ with the speech carefully prepared, the speaker needed to take a moment to gather his thoughts.

- A Though feel nervous
- B He felt nervous
- C Feeling nervous even
- D Despite his nervous

54 When you buy a new cell phone, _____ insurance in case of any accidents or theft.

- A it definitely would be worth
- B it's definitely worth getting
- C is worth it definitely
- D it's definitely worth to get

55 Three months _____ the first seeds, the tomatoes were ready to pick and eat.

- A earlier were planted
- B how did they plant it
- C ago they were planted
- D after having planted

56 _____ her professor's intervention, Sandra would have failed her final semester.

- A It could have helped
- B If only she had had
- C Not only had she had
- D Had it not been for

57 Prior to the accident, the car was moving erratically _____ there was some kind of problem.

- A even though suggesting
- B as if to suggest
- C which we suggest
- D that was to suggest

58 If I am _____ get this promotion, I'll do everything to ensure I succeed in the role.

- A as fortunate as I
- B most fortunate for
- C fortunate insofar as
- D so fortunate as to

| 51 | A | B | C | D | 52 | A | B | C | D | 53 | A | B | C | D | 54 | A | B | C | D |
| 55 | A | B | C | D | 56 | A | B | C | D | 57 | A | B | C | D | 58 | A | B | C | D |

Part 1 | Grammar | Test 1

59 I know it's more environmentally friendly to take the bus to work but _____ drive.

A rather would I
B I would sooner
C I'd far easier
D hardly had I

60 These two cars have virtually the same specification, but _____ is in the quality of materials used.

A they differ were
B they main difference
C what they different
D where they differ

61 The company is planning to move to that new _____ right by the train station downtown.

A fifteen-story building
B fifteen-stories building
C fifteen-stories buildings
D fifteen-storey buildings

62 He treats all the actors like dirt, so there is no way I am going to see _____.

A that play he has
B that play of his
C his play he has
D he has a play

63 _____ how air travel has changed the world and made it seem much smaller than it once was.

A Not only can we see
B Hardly can we see
C Seeing it is easy
D It's not hard to see

64 We know you _____ hard for this weekend's holiday, so General Stores is offering a 10% discount on everything.

A are to have prepared
B can only be preparing
C will have been preparing
D would have prepared

65 This park will be a valuable asset to all, with the added benefit _____ in collaboration with the citizens.

A that it has designed
B to it being designed
C of having been designed
D given for its design

66 _____ taxes even more, I dare say plenty of big businesses would move abroad.

A Not only did the government raise
B Were the government to raise
C Whether the government raises
D As the government has raised

This passage is about digital nomads.

The office job has remained remarkably **67)**_____ over time and generations of workers have trudged in and out of drab buildings at the same times, day in day out, for decades. Not anymore, however, as can be observed in the rise of the digital nomad.

Digital nomads work online and are **68)**_____ to work wherever they choose, as long as they can access the internet.

For some time now, younger generations of employees have been **69)**_____ the traditional office career. Being able to travel all over the world as a knowledge worker rather than working in the service industries is **70)**_____ attractive to those searching for adventure. This new breed of worker is **71)**_____ of life experiences rather than acquiring possessions.

Employers' attitudes are changing too. Whereas in the past people **72)**_____ this free spirit and expected young people to have a **73)**_____, nowadays companies understand that people **74)**_____ for freedom from the 9–5 job, and they are increasingly more flexible.

Obviously, the digital nomad existence is not for everyone, especially those who are not naturally **75)**_____. However, the **76)**_____ of this new approach on employment are vast and will continue to have an impact for the foreseeable future.

67	A	distinct	C	explicit
	B	constant	D	systematic

68	A	at liberty	C	at the best of times
	B	in no uncertain terms	D	in all likelihood

69	A	crying out for	C	getting caught up in
	B	resigning themselves to	D	turning their backs on

70	A	unanimously	C	wholeheartedly
	B	systematically	D	undeniably

71	A	in anticipation	C	in pursuit
	B	on the verge	D	on the brink

72	A	misinterpreted	C	implied
	B	frowned on	D	reproached

73	A	charity	C	vocation
	B	quest	D	discipline

74	A	long	C	pressure
	B	crave	D	treasure

75	A	mechanical	C	compatible
	B	persistent	D	self-reliant

76	A	implications	C	indications
	B	presumptions	D	associations

67	A	B	C	D
71	A	B	C	D
75	A	B	C	D

68	A	B	C	D
72	A	B	C	D
76	A	B	C	D

69	A	B	C	D
73	A	B	C	D

70	A	B	C	D
74	A	B	C	D

Part 2 | Multiple-choice Cloze | Test 1

This passage is about coral reefs.

Of all the Earth's ecosystems, the most **77)**_____ and under threat from climate change are the coral reefs. Although they make up a small part of the seabed, these precious marine environments **78)**_____ more than a quarter of ocean life and are fundamental to life in coastal communities, providing protection from storms and floods as well as coastal **79)**_____.

Unfortunately, many coral reefs have suffered significant **80)**_____ from 'bleaching', which is when the colorful algae that live inside the coral die, causing it to turn white. This happens because the coral is extremely sensitive and cannot **81)**_____ changes in sea temperature. An example of this is the Great Barrier Reef, where over half the coral has been **82)**_____ by bleaching, and it now **83)**_____ how it looked less than a decade ago.

84)_____, it is up to humans to adopt new ways of living that cause less damage to coral reefs. There are also calls for governments to work hard to **85)**_____ bad fishing practices, which contribute significantly to the destruction of coral reefs. Although the future may appear **86)**_____, some scientists are optimistic that we can reverse this trend and see corals thrive once more.

| 77 | A | elusive | C | fragile |
| | B | disturbed | D | marginal |

| 78 | A | work out | C | refer to |
| | B | take over | D | account for |

| 79 | A | erosion | C | inhibition |
| | B | isolation | D | fraction |

| 80 | A | devastation | C | deprivation |
| | B | interference | D | composition |

| 81 | A | dispute | C | withstand |
| | B | confront | D | submit |

| 82 | A | held off | C | torn down |
| | B | wiped out | D | cut back |

| 83 | A | has no parallel with | C | forms an analogy to |
| | B | bears little resemblance to | D | is a poor imitation of |

| 84 | A | Reportedly | C | Ironically |
| | B | Logically | D | Ultimately |

| 85 | A | crack down on | C | come up with |
| | B | fall back to | D | close in on |

| 86 | A | sceptical | C | negligible |
| | B | dubious | D | bleak |

87 I'm going to _____ the plans for the kitchen later today.

- **A** hold on
- **B** cut back
- **C** go by
- **D** look over

88 The investors pulled out of the skyscraper project at the last minute, and the architects' work went _____.

- **A** down the drain
- **B** over the hill
- **C** for the trash
- **D** out of shape

89 Despite the company's commitment to the environment, the changes they made were _____.

- **A** lenient
- **B** miniature
- **C** dubious
- **D** superficial

90 We had a constructive, _____ brief, meeting to clarify the design process.

- **A** whereby
- **B** regardless
- **C** albeit
- **D** insofar as

91 The movie _____ on for three hours without anything very remarkable happening.

- **A** dragged
- **B** scrambled
- **C** trailed
- **D** hung

92 Pre-election polls have a wide _____ of error, as voters are known to change their minds.

- **A** room
- **B** space
- **C** standard
- **D** margin

93 They weren't aiming to tell anyone about the pregnancy, but the news _____ during dinner.

- **A** slipped up
- **B** slipped out
- **C** slipped away
- **D** slipped through

94 Always add a _____ of fish sauce to a Thai-style curry to bring out the flavor.

- **A** grain
- **B** shred
- **C** dash
- **D** sip

95 Mr Cooper was _____ in how he dressed for work with freshly pressed suits and shirts.

- **A** frantic
- **B** meticulous
- **C** orthodox
- **D** spotless

96 The school works hard to deal with bad behavior, and only as a last _____ is exclusion an option.

- **A** resort
- **B** decree
- **C** corner
- **D** bet

97 In order to agree a trade deal, it takes a _____ effort from both sides.

- **A** preserved
- **B** persisted
- **C** sustained
- **D** retained

98 David wasn't a morning person, and often became _____ at the slightest bit of noise.

- **A** irrefutable
- **B** irritable
- **C** irrational
- **D** irresistible

99 When you _____ your mind back to the start of the year, could you imagine that you'd be married now?

- **A** bear
- **B** spring
- **C** set
- **D** cast

100 Karl was hoping he wouldn't put his _____ in his mouth during the interview.

- **A** hand
- **B** foot
- **C** elbow
- **D** head

101 The company wanted to _____ away from cell phones and tap into smartwatch market.

- **A** gamble
- **B** spread
- **C** issue
- **D** venture

102 The new campus block will be opened by _____ sociologist, Dr Leon Proudfoot.

- **A** eminent
- **B** superior
- **C** lofty
- **D** remarkable

This passage is about mealtimes.

Family mealtimes have been a mainstay of everyday cultural life in the USA for more than two centuries. While the central concept of sharing food with loved ones at the end of the working day still holds true for many American families, its development has followed the twists and turns of cultural change.

Dinnertime was first popularized in the USA during the 19th Century, and, as with many cultural traditions, it originated in Europe in the 18th Century as a result of changing work practices brought about by the Industrial Revolution. As more and more people were employed in factories, they began to shift their main mealtime from the middle of the day towards the evening since they weren't paid for the time they took to eat lunch. As time progressed, dinnertime became firmly entrenched in society, and as it evolved it created new behaviors. One of these was the expectation that the family dinnertime would be a pleasant experience focused on **ritual**, civilized conversation and polite manners. The suggestion was that it represented stability and an opportunity for families to become closer emotionally.

One of the first dining rooms in the USA was in Thomas Jefferson's house, and soon enough dining rooms appeared in wealthy homes and, subsequently, in all parts of society throughout the country. In 1950s America, the family dinnertime started to feature in popular entertainment such as movies and television, where it invariably showed a smiling nuclear family enjoying home-cooked food prepared by the mother. Seating arrangements were always the same, with fathers sitting at the head of the table, mothers opposite them and children either side, something that some social commentators believe reinforced narrow gender roles for several generations. In reality, the likelihood is that many mealtimes involved rows and moods that upset the happy atmosphere seen on screen.

103 What is the main purpose of the passage?
   A   to describe how work influenced family mealtimes
   B   to outline the evolution of 'dinnertime'
   C   to trace the origin of the word 'dinnertime'
   D   to explain why dinnertime is less popular nowadays

104 In the fifth sentence of paragraph 2, which word could best replace **ritual**?
   A   measurement
   B   practice
   C   presence
   D   rhythm

105 Why did workers change the time of day when they ate a large meal?
   A   They didn't like eating with colleagues.
   B   They wanted a shorter working day.
   C   They preferred to cook their own meals.
   D   They didn't have enough time for lunch.

106 According to the passage, what did family dinnertime influence?
   A   techniques for preparing food
   B   time spent on entertainment
   C   society's opinions of women
   D   how families communicated

107 What does the author imply?
   A   Images of family mealtimes had a negative impact on society.
   B   Sharing food together has improved people's diets.
   C   The benefits of family mealtimes outweigh the drawbacks.
   D   Most people do not enjoy mealtimes with their family.

Despite the fact that modern ways of working have impacted on mealtimes, a recent study reported that more than half of its participants maintained the tradition of eating their evening meal as a family. The contemporary twist is that they probably do not prepare the meals themselves. This may be one of the positive effects of food-ordering services, since they save time on food preparation and enable families to still take part in the conservational aspects of dinnertime. The sheer diversity of food that can be delivered to people's doors means families can look forward to mealtimes, even if for the food rather than the company!

108 What aspect of dinnertime has changed most recently?
- **A** topics that family members talk about
- **B** who is responsible for cooking meals
- **C** the range of meals people consume
- **D** attitudes towards eating as a family

103	A	B	C	D
107	A	B	C	D

104	A	B	C	D
108	A	B	C	D

105	A	B	C	D

106	A	B	C	D

This passage is about live music.

Everyone knows that attending a live music performance, whether a musical, a concert or a festival, is a magical experience. Live events are memorable because each one generates a unique essence or atmosphere that can never really be re-created by listening to a recorded version of the same music. But why exactly do people respond so emotionally to standing in front of their favorite singers and musicians on stage?

One suggestion is connected to the sense of community that runs deep in the human psyche. Humans have a deep-seated desire for shared physical experiences, and music accompanies language as a form of communication. Where words are used to transmit ideas and knowledge between individuals, music is often said to convey emotions.

When people come together to listen to and appreciate a musical performance, they are taking part in an intimate, emotional setting. This participation in musical rhythms makes their bodies feel good, and, by extension, puts them in a good mood. In fact, studies have shown that close friends frequently synchronize their movements when walking along the street together.

One interesting aspect of the shared musical experience is that people do not have to be dancing or moving together in a crowd to feel connected. In orchestral concerts and musicals, the audience is still, yet the music ebbs and flows with a certain structure. This has changes of pace, volume and tone, all of which generate a response that the audience will share as one.

It is worth mentioning that some cultures do not separate music from other sensory experiences (such as play, dance or communal cooperation in ceremonial events) in the way that western cultures do.

109 What is the main purpose of the passage?
   A to compare live music in different countries
   B to report on research into musical performances
   C to explore music as a common experience
   D to discuss the psychological effects of live music

110 In the first paragraph, how does the author describe live events?
   A They affect people differently.
   B They are deeply personal.
   C They are one of a kind.
   D They help people relax.

111 What does the author say about music and language?
   A They both communicate knowledge.
   B They complement each other.
   C They generate strong emotions.
   D They play similar social roles.

112 What have researchers discovered?
   A All humans respond emotionally to music.
   B Live music performances have health benefits.
   C Classical music has the biggest impact on emotions.
   D Human bonds and movement are connected.

113 What does the author say about live music performances?
   A The experience is enhanced by going with friends.
   B Dancing creates stronger emotional feelings.
   C If people are sitting down, they feel less connected.
   D Many types of live music create a common experience.

In fact, many cultures use the word for music to describe all of these activities, which encourage people to move together as one.

114 What point is the author making about non-western cultures?

   A   They interpret music more widely.
   B   They combine music and dance.
   C   They share musical activities more.
   D   They value live music more highly.

109	A	B	C	D
113	A	B	C	D

110	A	B	C	D
114	A	B	C	D

111	A	B	C	D

112	A	B	C	D

This passage is about teenagers.

When we think of teenagers there are many words that come to mind, such as 'rebellious', 'moody' and 'lazy' – words that are generally perceived as negative, especially by adults. These character **traits** are, however, simply products of the enormous changes taking place in teenagers' brains, changes that until recently were severely misunderstood. Previous generations of teenagers were labelled as difficult, immature or uncooperative when, in reality, they had little control over their behavior given their young age.

Over the last couple of decades, thanks to improved technology in the field of brain scanning, scientists are finally beginning to shed light on the teenage brain. Their discoveries are fascinating, not least because they demonstrate quite how wrong our assessment of teenagers' behavior has been in the past and how daily life can cause them much more distress than was ever imagined. One of the most important discoveries made is that melatonin, the hormone that regulates sleep cycles, rises and falls later in the day for teenagers, which accounts for their notorious morning sleepiness. Several high schools have implemented a later school day with the aim of improving the educational experience for both students and teachers, some of whom have since reported better engagement.

Other changes include higher levels of dopamine, the hormone that produces feelings of curiosity and pleasure, which explains typical teenagers' increased risk-taking and interest in new activities. In addition, mood swings can be attributed to sharp rises and falls in other hormones such as serotonin, as well as an increase in brain activity related to social interactions. It must also be recognized that adolescents are navigating a wealth of new experiences that they must try to understand, and this takes both time and effort.

115 What is the main purpose of the passage?
   A   to offer practical solutions
   B   to report on research
   C   to explore theoretical standpoints
   D   to argue for changes

116 In the second sentence of paragraph 1, which word could best replace **traits**?
   A   stances
   B   virtues
   C   deceptions
   D   attributes

117 What does the author say about teenagers in the past?
   A   Their behavior was worse.
   B   They were difficult to manage.
   C   They were unfairly assessed.
   D   They had better self-awareness.

118 What was a result of research into the teenage brain on education?
   A   The content of courses was changed.
   B   Schools adjusted their schedules.
   C   Teachers changed their methods.
   D   Extra afternoon classes were added.

119 Why are teenagers' moods so unpredictable?
   A   Their brains are overactive.
   B   There is a rise in a specific hormone.
   C   They have hormonal fluctuations.
   D   They have increased anxiety.

For example, adults may well conclude that teenagers who spend hours agonizing over why their best friend suddenly seems to hate them are being 'dramatic'. However, the reality is that this behavior is time well spent since it will contribute, ultimately, to of a set of essential skills in adult life, which, after all, is only a few years away.

120 What does the passage say about friendship problems?

    A Resolving them is complex.

    B They inform vital social skills.

    C Their impact is underestimated.

    D All teenagers experience them.

| 115 | A | B | C | D | | 116 | A | B | C | D | | 117 | A | B | C | D | | 118 | A | B | C | D |
| 119 | A | B | C | D | | 120 | A | B | C | D |

Reading ECPE
Test 2

51 They were stunned that the tickets near the stage _____ than those right at the back of the theatre.

  A were not any expensive
  B were not as expensive
  C were none so expensive
  D were no more expensive

52 _____ our mains when the server came along and snatched up the plates, telling us they were closing.

  A We had finished hardly
  B Had we finished hardly
  C Hardly had we finished
  D Finished hardly had we

53 _____ this product malfunctions, be sure to return it to the retailer for a refund or replacement.

  A In the event that
  B On condition when
  C So long as
  D Provided for

54 Rather than planning every minute detail of our vacation, why don't we just _____?

  A take it as it comes
  B take as comes it
  C take what it comes
  D take it to come

55 First Response Industries, _____, is a company that deals in emergency medical devices.

  A with its name implies
  B implying as its name
  C as the name implies
  D to imply the name

56 _____ disturb your mom when she's working in her office.

  A Don't be sure to
  B You're sure to not
  C To be sure don't
  D Be sure not to

57 Ellen couldn't find the book she was looking for, but she _____ a recommendation for similar one.

  A had been gotten
  B was getting
  C did get
  D has been getting

58 In order to process your application quickly, please bring _____ I requested to my office.

  A some papers that
  B the papers that
  C your papers what
  D a paper to which

Part 1 | Grammar | Test 2

59 We were all surprised when John quit because nobody _____ idea that he had any intention of leaving.

A didn't have a faint
B had the faintest
C had only a faint
D was having the faintest

60 Most young couples have to _____ a house until they've both got a stable income.

A hold buying off
B hold off on buying
C hold buying from
D hold from buy

61 They took on extra staff at the free concert _____ large crowds.

A that anticipating
B to anticipate some
C with anticipation for
D in anticipation of

62 We _____ in Los Angeles at 7:30am, but our flight was delayed.

A had due to arrive
B were due arriving
C were due to arrive
D had been due arriving

63 Nuria _____ her parents' car without asking beforehand.

A wouldn't dream of driving
B wouldn't dream to drive
C wouldn't have dreamt to drive
D wouldn't be dreaming of driving

64 The team is bound to win the track events as _____ super hard, but they are also really talented.

A not only have they been training
B they have been training not only
C not only they have been training
D they not only have trained

65 If the bosses aren't going to listen to your solutions, _____ their own mess.

A let them have fixed
B let them fix
C let fixing themselves
D let them to fix

66 _____, the farmers were already up and working in the fields.

A Before it is sunrise
B It was before sunrise
C Being before sunrise
D The sunrise happening

Reading ECPE

This passage is about Silicon Valley.

Silicon Valley is renowned as the home of countless **67)**_____ in all things technological. With famous corporations headquartered there and innovative starts ups on every corner, it is constantly **68)**_____ in all sorts of fields.

Yet few people are aware that its history is grounded more in academia than in business. The area gained prominence **69)**_____ of the 20th Century, after the establishment of Stanford University in 1891. This, coupled with an **70)**_____ of money and increasing international trade, soon created a unique business culture.

The second boost came during the 1950s from Stanford's dean of engineering, Frederick Terman, an academic who had **71)**_____ turning the area's electronics industry into an economic powerhouse. His approach was **72)**_____ on strict guidelines concerning what research the university would do for private organizations or government. He persuaded William Shockley, an innovator in transistor technology, into **73)**_____ and setting up a company, but, unfortunately, he was **74)**_____ at management and the company soon dissolved. However, the engineers from his company went on to set up Fairchild Semiconductors, which became remarkably successful. The new company had **75)**_____ Silicon Valley, and this is still felt today since almost three quarters of Bay Area companies are considered to be its direct **76)**_____.

67	A	protagonists	C	innovators
	B	intruders	D	advocates

68	A	breaking new ground	C	going with the flow
	B	turning over a new leaf	D	burning the midnight oil

69	A	on the dot	C	in the face
	B	at the turn	D	to the point

70	A	overload	C	outline
	B	expenditure	D	influx

71	A	set his sights on	C	taken stock of
	B	come to terms with	D	given rise to

72	A	addressed	C	founded
	B	related	D	represented

73	A	joining forces	C	breaking free
	B	knowing best	D	bearing fruit

74	A	deceptive	C	ruthless
	B	appalling	D	conceited

75	A	an intense significance in	C	a profound impact on
	B	deep indications for	D	sincere efforts in

76	A	hierarchies	C	predecessors
	B	ventures	D	descendants

67	A	B	C	D
71	A	B	C	D
75	A	B	C	D

68	A	B	C	D
72	A	B	C	D
76	A	B	C	D

69	A	B	C	D
73	A	B	C	D

70	A	B	C	D
74	A	B	C	D

This passage is about automation.

While automated vehicles seem like a vision that wouldn't look 77)_____ in a sci-fi movie, they are very much a reality in today's world. Citizens of cities like Austin, Pittsburgh and Phoenix, amongst others, are some of the 78)_____ already sharing their highways with fully driverless automobiles.

Naturally, all such considerable developments tend to bring about skepticism from the general public, especially regarding road safety, with many people 79)_____ of whether automation can really be as trustworthy as human control. However, the fact of the matter is that the data suggest 80)_____, as does history.

Developments that involve automation have always taken time for the public to 81)_____ themselves to. Nowadays, for example, we wouldn't think twice about using an automatic elevator, but at the 82)_____ of their automation many people felt 83)_____ about it, as they were accustomed to having an elevator 'driver' whose very presence provided a psychological 84)_____ to passengers.

Ironically, what many people don't appreciate is that human action is considerably more 85)_____ to errors compared to the reliability of automation. This has already been embraced in the aviation industry where some of the most demanding manoeuvres are 86)_____ automation, and before long, hopefully, a similar confidence will be bestowed on vehicle automation.

| 77 | A | out of place | C | back to front |
| | B | on the cards | D | a safe bet |

| 78 | A | founders | C | developers |
| | B | champions | D | pioneers |

| 79 | A | jumping to conclusions | C | keeping their fingers crossed |
| | B | posing the question | D | raising the alarm |

| 80 | A | it | C | to |
| | B | that | D | so |

| 81 | A | confront | C | reconcile |
| | B | prevail | D | incorporate |

| 82 | A | outset | C | application |
| | B | principle | D | means |

| 83 | A | in confidence | C | off limits |
| | B | ill at ease | D | touch and go |

| 84 | A | tolerance | C | reassurance |
| | B | resignation | D | willpower |

| 85 | A | legitimate | C | susceptible |
| | B | eminent | D | disposable |

| 86 | A | authorized by | C | made do with |
| | B | implied in | D | left to |

87 Worker _____ is especially important to the company, which is why we offer great employee benefits.

- A rejection
- B retention
- C resolution
- D repression

88 For Jane, the _____ of working in an office was something she wanted to avoid no matter what.

- A mediocrity
- B stability
- C humanity
- D peculiarity

89 Working in the movie industry can be very _____, but for the majority it's a tough business with little reward.

- A lucrative
- B immense
- C applicable
- D monetary

90 There was _____ in the community when the prisoner was released early.

- A rapture
- B sincerity
- C irony
- D outrage

91 As far as I'm concerned, this idea _____ serious consideration.

- A merits
- B endorses
- C appreciates
- D devises

92 When the cost of living rises, everyone has to _____.

- A toe the line
- B tighten their belts
- C make their way
- D recharge their batteries

93 If you _____ it, you'll master the guitar in a couple of years.

- A keep in
- B keep at
- C keep up
- D keep to

94 Nick was only _____ injured in the car accident, and was still able to go to work.

- A visibly
- B deeply
- C unavoidably
- D superficially

95 The statue was erected to _____ the achievements of the city's famous artist, Erika Jones.

- A reinforce
- B overlook
- C embody
- D commemorate

96 There are _____ drinks and snacks available on all AirGo long-haul flights.

- A supplementary
- B complimentary
- C mandatory
- D voluntary

97 Vicky moved to Canada and gradually _____ from her friends.

- A slipped away
- B stepped down
- C backed out
- D drifted apart

98 Whitez detergent is specially developed to avoid _____ on your family's skin.

- A irritations
- B annoyances
- C nuisances
- D frustrations

99 I noticed someone attempting to steal a car and had the _____ to call the police

- A means to an end
- B conscious decision
- C presence of mind
- D breadth of experience

100 Basil has a pleasant taste and _____ that can be sensed in any dish.

- A musk
- B air
- C odor
- D stink

101 My memories of living in southern France are something I will _____ forever.

- A treasure
- B perceive
- C indulge
- D deduce

102 Research suggests that people _____ giving speeches more than taking exams.

- A revolt
- B dread
- C suppress
- D disguise

This passage is about probiotics.

Probiotics seem to be all the rage in many parts of the USA at the moment, and understandably so – after all, who wouldn't want to take a one-size-fits-all solution to any health issues they might have? However, the jury still seems to be out regarding whether they can really live up to all the hype currently surrounding them.

What we can declare with some certainty is that our microbiome, in particular the microorganisms in the gut, is important to our health, and that the array of people's microbiomes in the West is becoming more and more limited due to antibiotics use and, **ironically**, the efforts we make to stay hygienic. As a result of this, conditions like asthma and allergies have soared in recent decades.

Probiotics claim to help populate the gut with healthy microorganisms, therefore improving overall gut health and possibly generating a curative effect for other illnesses. These kinds of probiotics are found naturally in many foods such as sauerkraut, but these are not in the everyday diet of many Westerners. More recently, as a result, probiotic juices, capsules and pills have been made so that people can take them consistently day to day, and this has grown into a multi-billion-dollar industry.

There are some factions out there that will categorically state that these probiotics can't make serious changes to our health, but the truth of their effects may well be more ambiguous. There is some evidence, for instance, that they can help sufferers of digestive illnesses related to the stomach, but the claims made that they could also help with a whole host of illnesses cannot be adequately validated at present. This doesn't mean that they can't – or indeed one day won't – have a positive effect on other ailments.

Firstly, there are trillions of microorganisms in the gut, and unlocking the formulae of these is not a simple endeavor that has been achieved, even partially. At the moment, while there is a bewildering range of probiotics in the market, their effectiveness is **arbitrary** in that any one person could take one brand and respond differently to someone else.

103 What is the main purpose of the passage?
- **A** to outline the uses of probiotics
- **B** to discuss the effectiveness of probiotics
- **C** to describe how probiotics function
- **D** to explain why the popularity of probitics has grown

104 What does the writer say about Westerners' gut health?
- **A** It's cleaner than it was.
- **B** It's more important than it used to be.
- **C** It's worse than before.
- **D** It has the most microbiomes.

105 In paragraph 2, which word could best replace **ironically**?
- **A** justifiably
- **B** scrupulously
- **C** acutely
- **D** paradoxically

106 What does the writer say about the effectiveness of probiotics?
- **A** They are the answer for people with gut problems.
- **B** They can help with a range of illnesses.
- **C** More validation studies need to be done.
- **D** They are limited in their benefits so far.

107 In the second sentence of paragraph 5, which word could best replace **arbitrary**?
- **A** unknown
- **B** random
- **C** varied
- **D** useless

Therefore, effectiveness now is up to individual trial and error, and it's up to the scientists to build upon what they already know to create more effective and targeted remedies for the future.

108 What is the writer's overall opinion of probiotics?

A They could be more effective once we know more about them.

B They are likely to replace traditional medicine one day.

C They should be studied more before they are sold.

D They don't make much difference to our overall health.

103	A	B	C	D
107	A	B	C	D

104	A	B	C	D
108	A	B	C	D

105	A	B	C	D

106	A	B	C	D

This passage is about the Brooklyn Bridge.

With their sweeping curves and imposing towers, suspension bridges are impressive and awe-inspiring structures, and the Brooklyn Bridge is one of the most iconic. Spanning the East River and connecting Brooklyn with the island of Manhattan, the Brooklyn Bridge was innovative in its use of materials being the first to use steel in place of iron. When it opened in 1884, it took the record for the longest suspension bridge in the world.

Despite the fact that the project was beset by all sorts of troubles, including the tragic death of its engineer, John Roebling, and costs that spiralled to $15 million (double the predicted amount), the bridge is nothing short of a triumph of engineering. Its completion was also a testament to the efforts made by Roebling's son Washington and daughter-in-law Emily who ensured that his vision was realized after his death.

The issues that Roebling had to overcome were sizeable and had therefore prevented a bridge from previously being constructed over the East River even though, for many years, the need for a crossing was plain for all to see. First and foremost was the river itself, which is actually more of a tidal estuary, extremely wide in many places with deep and turbulent water. Any bridge would have needed the deepest foundations ever built and to be able to withstand the pressures of tidal waters. Construction workers frequently suffered from decompression sickness, so working on a project such as this was dangerous. Compression sickness occurs when people move too quickly from a high-pressure to low-pressure environment, and typically affects underwater divers, and workers on construction sites on riverbeds or seabeds.

There were additional factors that the engineers had to account for, including the fact that the East River had more river traffic than almost any other stretch of water on Earth.

109 What is the main purpose of the passage?
- A to describe features of bridge engineering
- B to acknowledge the people who built the bridge
- C to explain the complexities of building the bridge
- D to show why people are attracted to the bridge

110 What does the passage say about the project?
- A it was completed on schedule
- B it received financial subsidies
- C it had some design flaws
- D it suffered several setbacks

111 What does the author say about the East River?
- A it was troublesome for vessels to navigate
- B its qualities are dissimilar to those of other rivers
- C it has few stretches suitable for bridges
- D its bed is not appropriate for heavy foundations

112 In the fourth sentence of paragraph 4, what does **these** refer to?
- A factors
- B implications
- C loads
- D towers

113 Why had no one built a bridge over the East River before?
- A raising sufficient investment was problematic
- B engineering practices were not advanced enough
- C the risk of accidents put many engineers off the idea
- D the need had not been sufficiently critical

For the river to remain unobstructed, any bridge would need to be high and long. This would then have implications for the towers, which would need to be strong enough to shoulder the enormous loads of the roadway and cables. All of **these** resulted in a challenge that was significantly beyond the expertise and experience of most engineers of the day.

However, Roebling's understanding of materials, and steel in particular, allowed him to propose a design that answered all the engineering questions associated with the Brooklyn Bridge, and to pave the way for a revolution in construction in fields as diverse as aviation, elevators and cable cars.

114 According to the passage, what was John Roebling's legacy?

  A his innovation had a lasting impact on industry
  B his bridge designs were copied extensively
  C he invented modern engineering practices
  D he made construction sites safer for workers

This passage is about technology.

Most people have some kind of love–hate relationship with technology that varies from being addicted to their phones to wanting to throw their malfunctioning printer out of the window. You'd be inhuman not to have these kinds of reactions sometimes. This kind of relationship can also be seen in the guest experience in hotel use, where most customers love high-tech convenience, but only up to a point.

Nowadays, the idea of hyper-personalization is all the rage for many hotel groups, which tailors the guest experience, from booking through to post-stay follow ups, according to the needs and personalities of individual guests. **This** puts the customer experience at the forefront by using customer data, such as browsing activities and purchasing behavior, to ensure that hotels offer exactly what every customer needs.

This is all well and good, but hotels must not lose sight of the customer when drawn into this data-driven technology. While studies indicate that the majority of hotel guests find the use of technology to do things such as order room service a welcome advancement from the more traditional face-to-face exchanges, a large proportion also said that they feel the need for human interaction should they face any technological problems during their stay. Indeed, many forms of digital assistance, such as self-help screens, FAQs or chat bots, are generally cited by guests as irritations. Despite often doing so, hotels should not neglect the customer who would prefer their entire guest journey to be a genuine, human experience. There could be a myriad of reasons for this: perhaps the guest is constantly on the computer or phone and requires a digital detox; or perhaps, for them, technology has passed them by.

Providing a seamless, dual process of guest interaction is something that many hotels now need to focus on, and data indicates support for this assertion. Recent research has found that some chains had overly focused on their digital offering at the expense of the personal touch that comes from human interaction.

115 What is the main purpose of the passage?
- A to explain why technology is important in the hotel industry
- B to argue how hotels should deploy technology
- C to describe the problems guests have with technology
- D to outline the types of technology hotels use

116 In paragraph 2, sentence 2, what does **this** refer to?
- A the needs and personalities of guests
- B the experience of the customer
- C booking and post-stay follow ups
- D the idea of hyperpersonalization

117 What does the writer say about hyperpersonalization?
- A Not everybody enjoys personalized experiences.
- B It can distract from real customer service
- C It can only be as good as the data that is available.
- D It is overwhelmingly successful for hotels.

118 What do hotels have a tendency to do?
- A overestimate their customers' technological abilities
- B overlook part of their customer base
- C undersell technological innovation
- D undervalue the guest journey

119 In paragraph 4, sentence 3, which expression could replace **the bottom line**?
- A the tip of the iceberg
- B the deciding factor
- C the prime example
- D the last resort

There is no denying that the world is advancing, and as such hotels need to keep up digitally, but **the bottom line** of all this is that they must also remember that the application of this technology at the right time is paramount, and that it should be done in conjunction with a human touch.

120 What does the writer think is the most important part of applying technology in hotels?

- A understanding the effects
- B knowing the limits
- C smoothing out problems
- D timing the changes

115	A	B	C	D
119	A	B	C	D

116	A	B	C	D
120	A	B	C	D

117	A	B	C	D

118	A	B	C	D

Reading ECPE
Test 3

51 Online privacy is _____ a solution is unlikely to present itself anytime soon.

   A a complex issue of which
   B so complex an issue that
   C too much a complex issue for
   D an issue so complex so

52 Andrea has been offered a job in Chicago, and everyone thinks _____ it.

   A she will be crazy if not taking
   B she'd be crazy for not taking
   C she'd be crazy not to take
   D she is crazy if she's not to take

53 Remember that during the exam if you _____, you will be found out and disqualified.

   A are resorting to cheat
   B had resorted to cheating
   C resort to cheating
   D resort to cheat

54 The discovery of a new planet _____ everything we thought we knew about the solar system.

   A has cast doubt on
   B casted doubt on
   C cast to doubt on
   D has doubted on

55 _____, when the fire alarm sounded, and the students had to vacate the room.

   A Hardly the lecture begun
   B The lecture hardly had begun
   C Hardly had the lecture begun
   D The lecture hardly begun

56 Most people had _____ after his last movie, but I think this one shows what a good director he can be.

   A written off
   B written him off
   C written off him
   D written his off

57 As far as I'm concerned, _____ company should be allowed to pollute the environment.

   A no one of a
   B none of any
   C not a one
   D not a single

58 The sheriff, _____ conflict resolution, talked the men out of fighting.

   A having been trained in
   B had been trained for
   C with being trained at
   D who has trained over

59 It doesn't matter _____ Brad agrees, we have no choice but to sell up and move.

   A if yes or not
   B whether or not
   C that whether
   D why or why not

60 _____ noticed that they add one or two extra things on the check that shouldn't be there.

   A Have I many times
   B Many times have I
   C A time many I have
   D Many a time have I

61 _____, the project would need a considerable amount of investment.

   A If it would to succeed
   B If it had succeeded
   C If it was to have succeeded
   D If it were to succeed

62 I'm shopping more at my local grocery store as I _____ them go out of business.

   A would hate seeing
   B would hate having seen
   C would be hating to see
   D would hate to see

63 According to our research, _____ that most people's fears tend to grow as they age.

   A it may be generalizing
   B it is to be generalized
   C it may be generalized
   D it may being generalized

64 Speed limits in the city centre are decreasing _____ the new safety campaign.

   A as in line
   B in line with
   C to the line off
   D for line to

65 We'll welcome any friend of yours to have Thanksgiving at our table, _____.

   A whoever might they be
   B whoever they might be
   C might they be whoever
   D they might whoever be

66 I wish kids played _____ when we were out on the street from dawn till dusk.

   A like used to us
   B as did we
   C as we used to
   D like did us

This passage is about procrastination.

Putting off important tasks, or 'procrastination' as it is commonly called, is something that we are all guilty of to a greater or lesser extent. How many of us, when faced with a demanding task, suddenly feel an **67)**_____ urge to clean the bathroom or reorder our bookshelves?

However, **68)**_____ to popular belief, the root of procrastination is not laziness or an unwillingness to do certain tasks, but a form of emotional management. The emotions **69)**_____ are always negative and are usually **70)**_____ by the thought of specific tasks.

Psychologists have begun to understand more about procrastination recently, and studies have **71)**_____ that it is related to regulating emotions rather than time management. Eliminating present bad moods is a far more urgent **72)**_____ for the human brain than attending to things that will affect us in the distant future. The human brain has evolved to give priority to **73)**_____ tasks, and therefore has an **74)**_____ for procrastination.

Apparently, our brains are just not **75)**_____ striking items off our 'to do' lists, which explains why everyone has a tendency to procrastinate. So, the next time you're not in the **76)**_____ an irritating task, remember that your brain is in control, and that you have little chance of overriding its decisions.

67	A	irresistible	C	industrious
	B	artificial	D	elaborate

68	A	adverse	C	conflicting
	B	at odds	D	contrary

69	A	at issue	C	on hand
	B	in question	D	at length

70	A	raised	C	wrecked
	B	provoked	D	outraged

71	A	maintained	C	leaked
	B	pleaded	D	revealed

72	A	stance	C	engagement
	B	administration	D	undertaking

73	A	accessible	C	imminent
	B	dynamic	D	physical

74	A	immediate scope	C	innate capacity
	B	unprecedented extent	D	overwhelming range

75	A	caught up in	C	flooded with
	B	cut out for	D	intent on

76	A	mood for	C	vicinity of
	B	interest in	D	process of

This passage is about otters.

When most people think of otters, the image that **77)**_____ is often one of adorable fluffy creatures that star in many a cute online video, but what many people don't know is that the sea otter is also **78)**_____ to maintaining ecosystems around coastal seabeds and in estuaries, in turn making them an **79)**_____ asset in wider environmental conservation.

Otters have a **80)**_____ appetite, and eat almost a quarter of their body weight each day to maintain warmth, with their **81)**_____ food source being the sea urchin. By managing the sea urchin population in this way, otters are inadvertently protecting the sea kelp, which urchins often consume. Sea kelp provides the dual benefit of offering **82)**_____ to a variety of sea creatures as well as reducing levels of carbon dioxide.

Unfortunately, the future of these ecosystems now **83)**_____. Otters have become relatively endangered, having been hunted for much of the 18th and 19th centuries, and, while there is now **84)**_____ in many places that protects otter populations specifically, the effects of centuries of hunting are **85)**_____, with many coastal areas virtually **86)**_____.

77	A	sets the ball rolling	C	is in the same boat
	B	springs to mind	D	catches your eye

78	A	fundamental	C	consistent
	B	exceptional	D	definitive

79	A	innumerable	C	indispensable
	B	inconceivable	D	irreversible

80	A	formidable	C	respectable
	B	thriving	D	resilient

81	A	prominent	C	supplementary
	B	paramount	D	staple

82	A	relief	C	refuge
	B	strength	D	settlement

83	A	gets out of hand	C	falls into place
	B	comes to light	D	hangs in the balance

84	A	delegation	C	allocation
	B	legislation	D	instruction

85	A	beyond dispute	C	in a big way
	B	on no account	D	beside the point

86	A	deceased	C	barren
	B	bland	D	negligent

87 Adam's parents wanted him to study law, but he didn't have the _____ to do so, and decided to give up college and travel.

- **A** inclination
- **B** anticipation
- **C** concession
- **D** intuition

88 She _____ her identity by wearing a wig and sunglasses.

- **A** misinterpreted
- **B** twisted
- **C** surrendered
- **D** concealed

89 Nevada is one of the most _____ populated states of the USA.

- **A** vaguely
- **B** vitally
- **C** scarcely
- **D** sparsely

90 That old building will be _____ to make way for a new library.

- **A** torn down
- **B** shaken off
- **C** taken over
- **D** mounted up

91 Several weeks had _____ and I still hadn't had a reply to my complaint letter.

- **A** dragged
- **B** elapsed
- **C** lingered
- **D** eroded

92 My parents _____ to make my friends feel welcome when they visit.

- **A** put their foot down
- **B** come to the rescue
- **C** make their presence felt
- **D** go out of their way

93 Most people just throw away apple _____ but they make great bird feed!

- **A** stones
- **B** hearts
- **C** stems
- **D** cores

94 Auditions will be held tonight for the male _____ in the play.

- **A** head
- **B** lead
- **C** front
- **D** chief

95 There is extra bed _____ in the cupboards should it be required.

   A fiber
   B cloth
   C linen
   D wear

96 By keeping your problems _____, you can maintain a positive attitude.

   A in essence
   B in attendance
   C in isolation
   D in perspective

97 Bob Duncan will be the _____ CEO while the vacancy is being advertised.

   A imperative
   B intact
   C interim
   D inherent

98 The airline upgraded us to first class to _____ for the six-hour delay.

   A compensate
   B gesture
   C intervene
   D appeal

99 Animals that live in polar regions have to be able to _____ the extreme cold.

   A wield
   B plead
   C tolerate
   D execute

100 I'd _____ the chance to live somewhere with a warm climate.

   A leap at
   B hold onto
   C dive into
   D bounce back

101 After he lost his job, Tom became very _____ and stopped meeting up with his usual group of friends.

   A withdrawn
   B restrained
   C bashful
   D modest

102 Employees of both companies were worried that their jobs might be affected by the _____.

   A fusion
   B merger
   C blend
   D sequence

This passage is about an art robbery.

On 18th March 1990, two men entered the Isabella Stewart Gardner Museum in Boston and committed a crime that has since been labelled the world's biggest art heist. They stole over five-hundred-million dollars' worth of paintings, none of which has been recovered in the thirty years since. Remarkably, during this time, nobody has come forward to claim the $10 million reward for information leading to the safe recovery of any of the items.

As art heist's go, it was not the most challenging given that among the city's criminals the museum was known for its absence of security measures. During its heyday in the early 20th Century, when Isabella Stewart Gardner was alive, the museum was known for its haphazard layout and lack of information about any of the exhibits. Apparently, this was all part of her design, so much so that when she died her will stated that the museum was to be preserved in its current state forever. This partly accounts for the loopholes in the building's security as the will prevented it from being modernized and taking advantage of improvements in technology.

On the night in question, posing as policeman responding to a potential disturbance, the thieves convinced the security guards to open the door. From then it was a simple matter of tying up the inexperienced guards and helping themselves to the museum's treasures. Despite the fact that the FBI identified a number of suspects, no one was ever brought to trial, and all the suspects have since passed away. As such the crime remains unsolved and has taken on an air of mystery, so much so that a documentary movie was recently made covering the whole investigation.

103 What is the main purpose of the passage?
 A to describe an unsolved crime
 B to show police investigation methods
 C to explain how a robbery happened
 D to explore motives for art heists

104 What did the museum's owner specify?
 A Items to add to the collection in the future.
 B That the museum remain unchanged.
 C To reorganize the arrangement of the exhibits
 D A thorough review of the security measures.

105 What does the author imply about the heist?
 A It was bound to happen sooner or later.
 B The police did not investigate thoroughly.
 C It could easily have been prevented.
 D The perpetrators were experienced criminals.

106 What sparked the making of a movie about the heist?
 A The flaws in the investigation.
 B The lack of a conviction.
 C The death of the suspects.
 D The value of the stolen items.

107 According to the passage, what is surprising about the heist?
 A An extremely valuable painting was not taken.
 B The guards were overpowered easily.
 C No one has claimed the reward for information.
 D The police could not identify any buyers.

One of the points that emerged from the investigation was that it was difficult to identify a motive for the heist. While one of the paintings was valued at $250 million, the most valuable piece in the museum was left untouched and the rest of the stolen items did not form a cohesive set. Often connections between stolen artworks from the same museum can shed light on who stole them and the potential buyers, yet in this case no such information was available. Today, there is some speculation that the less valuable items may well be in someone's home, although the location of the expensive items is anyone's guess.

108 What is a typical feature of art robberies?

A Specific paintings are targeted based on their value.

B The thieves often have possible buyers in mind.

C Stolen items are kept in a variety of locations.

D A theme usually links the stolen works of art.

| 103 | A | B | C | D |
| 107 | A | B | C | D |

| 104 | A | B | C | D |
| 108 | A | B | C | D |

| 105 | A | B | C | D |

| 106 | A | B | C | D |

This passage is about altitude sickness.

Altitude sickness affects people walking or climbing at altitudes of more than 8,000 feet, which is why it also known as 'mountain sickness'. Due to a drop in atmospheric pressure, the air at this height and above contains less oxygen, and this causes a reduction in the levels of oxygen in the blood too.

Altitude sickness has a range of symptoms, including headaches, nausea, shortness of breath and muscle aches. Some of these can be alleviated by medication, but this is usually unnecessary. For the most part, it is not a life-threatening condition, and sufferers report that symptoms gradually lessen over a few days as they become accustomed to the conditions.

It is worth highlighting that altitude sickness can affect anyone, irrespective of their level of fitness, including professional athletes. In fact, the fitter people are, the more likely they are to suffer from it, which seems counterintuitive. Trainers suggest that this could be because fit people generally push themselves too hard too quickly, and therefore, by not acclimatising themselves slowly to the lack of oxygen available in the environment, they are more vulnerable.

The identification and naming of altitude sickness is usually attributed to the French physiologist Paul Bert and his landmark 1878 book in which he described the condition. There was a lot of curiosity about the climatic conditions of high altitude in the 18th and 19th centuries, as this was a time when mountaineering and expeditions to remote places were popular. Many explorers such as Alexander von Humboldt and Horace-Bénédict de Saussure wrote in their diaries (with a certain amount of surprise) about breathing and movement difficulties.

More recently, research has shown that another Frenchman, Denis Jourdanet,

109 What is the main purpose of the passage?
- **A** to compare theories about altitude sickness
- **B** to describe where altitude sickness occurs
- **C** to give advice on dealing with altitude sickness
- **D** to clarify facts relating to the discovery of altitude sickness.

110 What does the writer say about the link between athletes and altitude sickness?
- **A** It is random.
- **B** It is permanent.
- **C** It is logical.
- **D** It is unexpected.

111 How should people tackle altitude sickness?
- **A** allow some time to adjust
- **B** prepare for it with a trainer
- **C** seek medical treatment
- **D** do a little gentle exercise

112 What fuelled 19th-century scientists' interest in altitude sickness?
- **A** an increase in the number of cases
- **B** research in climate at high altitudes
- **C** explorers' accounts of the condition
- **D** a new publication on the topic

113 In the final sentence of paragraph 5, what does the phrase **to his credit** mean?
- **A** He was a trustworthy person.
- **B** He had a good reputation.
- **C** He should be applauded.
- **D** He received some compensation.

probably discovered the condition several years prior to Paul Bert. Jourdanet was a doctor who lived in various places of differing altitudes in Mexico where he analyzed the effects of the altitudes on his wife's tuberculosis. He later returned to Paris and, in 1859, he published, to mixed reviews, his findings on the topic of air quality. A few years later he met Bert, and together they continued their research. **To his credit**, Paul Bert always acknowledged that Jourdanet's findings preceded his. However, history seems to have forgotten his valuable contribution to this aspect of scientific research.

114 What does the passage say about Denis Jourdanet?

    A   He used unconventional methods.

    B   He deserves wider recognition.

    C   His research was initially ignored.

    D   He collaborated with his wife.

This passage is about false hair.

Many people consider toupées and wigs to be a regular butt of jokes or source of embarrassment, opinions that are reinforced in many forms of entertainment, with cartoons and comedy often featuring falling hairpieces and the ensuing embarrassment. However, these head coverings have always played functional and emotional roles in many people's lives.

Wigs originated in Ancient Egypt, thousands of years ago. Both men and women at this time used to shave their heads to avoid lice, and their wigs shielded their heads from the sun. Similarly, in 16th- and 17th-century Europe, wigs were a commonplace feature of upper-class life. To avoid infestations of the hair, many aristocrats shaved their heads and wore an artificial hair equivalent.

While the popularity of wigs somewhat reduced in the 19th and 20th centuries, toupées, which cover only a small part of the head and are often worn by males, became common, certainly in Western cultures. This rise in popularity was due to an attitude shift where wider society started to view older men as less relevant and appealing, rather than past attitudes which saw age as a symbol of power and wisdom. This meant that men wanted to conceal their advancing years, and toupées aided in that. In fact, toupée use in the USA grew until around 1950 when more than 350,000 American men wore these hairpieces.

Despite the changing fortunes of both wigs and toupées, the production of both still accounts for a multi-billion-dollar industry. Whereas the toupée still has some **stigma** attached, the wig seems to have avoided this in recent history. There are also some examples of wigs being seen as status symbols throughout the world. For example, in some countries they are still used by the legal profession. And in the world of entertainment, they are seen as one of the pinnacles of style reinvention, and something to flaunt, unlike toupées, whose famous wearers tend to not advertise **the fact**.

115 What is the main purpose of the passage?
- A to explain people's attitudes about wigs and toupées
- B to compare the popularity of wigs and toupées
- C to describe the development of wigs and toupées
- D to highlight the practicalities of wigs and toupées

116 Why did people wear wigs in the past?
- A for status
- B for hygiene
- C for vanity
- D for warmth

117 Why did toupees become popular?
- A for reasons of vanity
- B to show social status
- C so men appeared richer
- D to hide any illnesses

118 What does the writer say about the popularity of wigs and toupees over time?
- A it has grown
- B it is unknown
- C it is reducing
- D it has fluctuated

119 In paragraph 4, sentence 2, which word could replace **stigma**?
- A shame
- B pity
- C secrecy
- D disgust

120 What does **the fact** refer to in the final line?

- **A** having a bald patch
- **B** wearing a hairpiece
- **C** flaunting themselves
- **D** working in entertainment

115	A	B	C	D
119	A	B	C	D

116	A	B	C	D
120	A	B	C	D

117	A	B	C	D

118	A	B	C	D

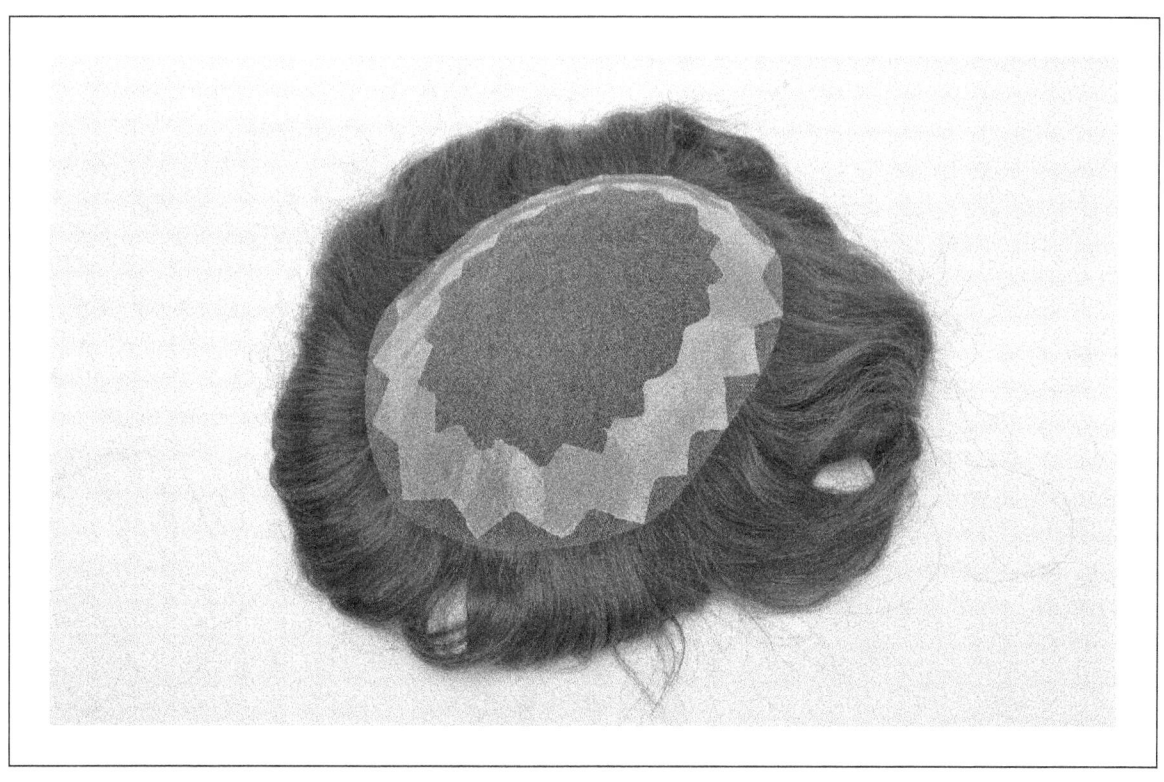

Reading ECPE
Test 4

51 You might want to take the bus to college, but it's _____ than walking.

- A none more quickly
- B much less quickly
- C not that much quicker
- D no anymore quicker

52 Everybody _____ doubts themselves when it comes to new responsibilities at work.

- A one time after another
- B some more another time
- C at one time or another
- D for some time or another

53 _____ five minutes earlier, I would have caught my connecting flight.

- A Were the plane to land
- B Had the plane landed
- C If the plane lands
- D Whether the plane landed

54 My cat _____ dead birds outside the front door and I can't stand it!

- A has always left
- B is being left
- C does always leave
- D is always leaving

55 The sales team _____ their targets because I hear they haven't received any bonuses this year.

- A couldn't have reached
- B couldn't be reaching
- C couldn't had reached
- D couldn't to be reached

56 Maria had been _____ her grandfather since he taught her how to tie her shoelaces.

- A with awe for
- B in awe of
- C with awe of
- D in awe with

57 The United Nations is a widely respected organization, _____ maintain international peace and security.

- A to which purpose is
- B which purposes for
- C which is the purpose to
- D the purpose of which is to

58 If the town hall doesn't _____ soon, we'll have no New Year's Day parade this year.

- A act it together
- B get an act together
- C get together to act
- D get its act together

59 _____ any problems completing your booking, please use the chat box for help.

- A Should you had
- B Should you be having
- C Should you have
- D Should you do have

60 Bob knew he _____ before the road trip, but he wasn't sure if he'd had enough time.

- A had his car servicing
- B should be serviced his car
- C had to have his car serviced
- D should get serviced his car

61 It _____ to write a novel in your spare time, especially as a single mother.

- A mustn't to have been easy
- B mustn't been easy
- C mustn't had been easy
- D mustn't have been easy

62 What the Buffalo Raiders have got to do now is _____ and think about the rest of the season.

- A put their loss to one side
- B put to aside the loss
- C put their losing aside
- D put losing at one side

63 When it came to the end of the tour, _____ of the band was talking to each other.

- A not a single member
- B none one member
- C were not any member
- D no single member

64 The residents of this community _____ loud noise after dark.

- A are not kind about
- B don't take kindly to
- C don't have kindness for
- D won't feel kindly that

65 The Empire State Building is _____ this country has ever seen.

- A as great an architectural feat as
- B great an architectural feat that
- C a great architectural feat as
- D this great architectural feat which

66 I thought I'd enjoy this history class, but _____ it.

- A I don't like really
- B I'm not really liking
- C I don't really like
- D I'm really not liking

59	A	B	C	D
63	A	B	C	D

60	A	B	C	D
64	A	B	C	D

61	A	B	C	D
65	A	B	C	D

62	A	B	C	D
66	A	B	C	D

This passage is about mosquitos.

The **67)**_____ mosquito, often simply considered a pest we have to **68)**_____ in hotter climates, is actually the world's deadliest creature, killing **69)**_____ a million people worldwide every year. What might seem like a harmless bite can often lead to serious complications in some parts of the world, with mosquitoes **70)**_____ a number of diseases to their hosts. They've even been cited as changing the **71)**_____ of history, killing Alexander the Great, halting the takeover of the Roman empire in Scotland, and contributing to the result of the American War of Independence.

The effects of mosquito bites may lead us to consider that, as these insects spread such deadly disease, they are worthy candidates for **72)**_____. While efforts have been made to minimize mosquito-borne diseases, the **73)**_____ of the natural world is the answer to why we don't do more. Mosquitos are part of the food chain, and they act as pollinators for plants and grasses. The **74)**_____ caused as a consequence of taking one species out of this network may cause unintended, and perhaps disastrous, results.

In addition, while we might **75)**_____ mosquitos to be a blight now, they may still have many unknown qualities that we have **76)**_____ discover, and that may be essential for the future of the human race.

67	A	fearful	C	petty
	B	feeble	D	humble

68	A	drive out	C	grin and bear
	B	stand up to	D	hold at bay

69	A	not least	C	the height of
	B	upwards of	D	in part

70	A	unloading	C	surpassing
	B	conceding	D	transmitting

71	A	course	C	field
	B	route	D	record

72	A	slaughter	C	eradication
	B	crackdown	D	prosecution

73	A	complexity	C	constraint
	B	ambiguity	D	dependence

74	A	upper limit	C	frame of mind
	B	knock-on effects	D	turn of events

75	A	caution	C	deem
	B	infer	D	diagnose

76	A	so to	C	thereafter to
	B	together to	D	yet to

Part 2 | Multiple-choice Cloze | Test 4

This passage is about the saxophone.

Most musical instruments around today were developed over hundreds (or, in the case of wooden flutes, thousands) of years. The saxophone is unlike any other instrument, given that its relatively recent invention can be 77)_____ just one individual. 78)_____ by Adolphe Sax in the 1840s, it was designed to 79)_____ qualities of both woodwind and brass instruments.

The saxophone is played with a reed, which means it is classified as a woodwind instrument 80)_____ a brass instrument, even though its appearance suggests otherwise. It failed to catch on, initially, as an orchestral instrument, but from the 1920s 81)_____ it started featuring in the American jazz scene, and with the 82)_____ of the Swing Era a decade later, the saxophone soon became 83)_____ popular.

Its primary feature is that it sounds good playing almost every genre of music, and the fact that it is so 84)_____ has meant that it has been able to 85)_____ changes in musical styles over the last century. From powerful solos in pop classics to warm harmonies in smooth jazz and everything in between, there is no doubt that the saxophone has 86)_____ musical history well beyond the shores of the USA.

77	A	developed by	C	formulated with
	B	attributed to	D	assembled by

78	A	Registered	C	Refined
	B	Unfolded	D	Conceived

79	A	be in line with	C	bring out the best
	B	have the edge over	D	make allowances for

80	A	long before	C	yet another
	B	at any rate	D	as opposed to

81	A	ahead	C	forth
	B	onwards	D	beyond

82	A	arrival	C	opening
	B	transmission	D	liberation

83	A	wildly	C	unanimously
	B	naturally	D	infinitely

84	A	faultless	C	versatile
	B	resourceful	D	coherent

85	A	come out of	C	lead up to
	B	go through with	D	keep up with

86	A	taken exception to	C	made way for
	B	got its hands on	D	left its mark on

77	A	B	C	D
81	A	B	C	D
85	A	B	C	D

78	A	B	C	D
82	A	B	C	D
86	A	B	C	D

79	A	B	C	D
83	A	B	C	D

80	A	B	C	D
84	A	B	C	D

87 We got the whole team to _____ and bought Oliver a great retirement gift.

A close in
B butt in
C chip in
D stand in

88 Scientists can learn a lot from _____ people's health over long periods of time.

A spreading
B tracking
C exhibiting
D displaying

89 The thieves got away with a _____ of over $3 million in jewellery.

A haul
B herd
C hike
D heap

90 Harry looked in on his son at 7pm, and he was still _____ asleep.

A quick
B soon
C fast
D full

91 Poor blood _____ can be identified by coldness in the extremities, especially the feet.

A rotation
B revolution
C motion
D circulation

92 There was a _____ breeze in the air when Paul took the dog out in the morning.

A rigid
B thick
C firm
D stiff

93 Poor sales have _____ the company's chances of making a profit this year.

A taken stock of
B cast doubt on
C made light of
D paid tribute to

94 Sarah didn't enjoy the movie because it was only a _____ adaptation of the book.

A free
B loose
C soft
D light

95 Students can only be excused for class on medical _____ or family emergencies.

   A grounds
   B intents
   C footings
   D notions

96 Law-enforcement officers must ensure that no details _____ their attention in an investigation.

   A escape
   B defy
   C leak
   D retreat

97 Nathan was _____ all day until the school called with his exam results.

   A on the line
   B on the side
   C on edge
   D on occasion

98 The principal _____ the students who had misbehaved to her office for an explanation.

   A rendered
   B contracted
   C summoned
   D alerted

99 Several vegan restaurants have recently _____ around town.

   A settled down
   B sprung up
   C come in
   D burst out

100 This opening event pays _____ to everyone who donated money to build this theatre.

   A tribute
   B regard
   C praise
   D consent

101 I haven't had these shoes for long, and they've _____ already.

   A sealed
   B split
   C scrapped
   D snatched

102 It can be difficult to resist the _____ to snack between meals when trying to diet.

   A intuition
   B incentive
   C insight
   D impulse

This passage is about salt.

Despite its unassuming appearance, salt has shaped many aspects of humanity's development over the centuries. All mammals, including humans, need salt for a number of bodily functions. This means that they need to eat food that is rich in salt. As humans moved from hunter gatherers to live in agricultural societies, they swapped a meat diet rich in salt for one based on vegetables and cereals. Consequently, there was a need to supplement their new plant-based diet. This naturally resulted in salt collection becoming a prominent feature of human life.

Almost every civilization has evidence of salt production, which demonstrates its importance. Archaeologists believe that humans in the Far East were the first to begin gathering salt as early as 6,000 BCE. Other great civilizations, including the Egyptians and Romans, followed suit, using salt as a way to preserve food and as a form of currency. Consequently, trading routes soon began to spread around the globe. Its uses started to go beyond food, too, and it was incorporated into various manufacturing processes such as paper making, dyeing textiles and making cleaning products, including soaps. In fact, salt is still widely used across the chemical industry today.

Its past status can be better understood by noting that many cities were able to amass vast **reserves** of wealth as a result of salt trading, cities such as Venice, Timbuktu and Salzburg (the latter being, literally, the 'city of salt'). The economic importance of salt also allowed leaders to impose salt taxes in order to raise revenues for industrial expansion, and wars occurred as international trade developed over time. In addition, salt-producing areas and cities were able to assist with specific infrastructure projects. In the USA a notable example of this is the Eerie Canal, which connects the Atlantic Ocean to the great lakes.

103 What is the main purpose of the passage?
- A to compare the uses of salt in different civilisations
- B to show how salt contributed to economic development
- C to describe the history of salt mining
- D to explain how collecting salt has changed over time

104 Why did humans start gathering salt?
- A for social reasons
- B to use as medicine
- C for economic reasons
- D to improve their diet

105 What does the passage say about the use of salt in industry?
- A It has been replaced by other methods.
- B It is no longer used in food production.
- C It is better than using man-made chemicals.
- D It remains relevant in manufacturing.

106 In the first sentence of paragraph 3, which word could best replace **reserves**?
- A stocks
- B means
- C provisions
- D assets

107 What is the Eerie Canal an example of?
- A a successful way of transporting salt across the USA
- B how the salt industry made a city famous
- C the wealth created by the salt industry
- D a route for trading salt internationally

Over half the cost of its construction was funded by the lucrative salt industry in the nearby city of Syracuse.

108 What does the author suggest about the impact of salt on human history?

   A   It has been a constant feature.
   B   It was more obvious in the past.
   C   It has grown over time.
   D   It was larger in some countries.

103	A	B	C	D
107	A	B	C	D

104	A	B	C	D
108	A	B	C	D

105	A	B	C	D

106	A	B	C	D

This passage is about space.

Apparently, there has never been a better time to study space due to the gigantic technological leaps the world's space agencies have taken in recent times. This, coupled with a new age of international cooperation, has caused astronomers, astrophysicists and cosmologists to become excited about their work in a way not seen since the golden days of space exploration in the mid-twentieth century.

The jewel in the crown of this shift in the field is the James Webb Space Telescope. Launched fourteen years after its original schedule, and at a cost of $10 billion (roughly twenty times over budget), it is the most ambitious, technically complex and costly telescope ever constructed. This technology enables the telescope to peer billions of years back into the past, something that its predecessors were unable to do. It is hoped that the James Webb Space Telescope will reveal details about how the first galaxies formed and shed light on some of astronomy's biggest questions about the origins of the universe, as well as posing new puzzles for future generations of space scientists.

One recent, fascinating discovery is the largest comet ever observed in space. Comets are large objects made from ice and dust, which astronomers are keen to understand more fully, believing that they contain clues about the formation of the solar system. Unfortunately, studying them is notoriously difficult because they typically inhabit the far reaches of the solar system. Astronomers found the comet quite by chance whilst looking for a completely different type of object in images from a telescope in Chile. They were surprised by the unexpected finding but were delighted by how useful it is likely to prove to the field. What makes this comet so special is that, by spotting it early in its journey, astronomers now have plenty of time to make further observations.

109 What is the main purpose of the passage?
- A to welcome a new era of research
- B to explain the importance of technology
- C to recommend future space research
- D to encourage people to become astronomers

110 What do scientists expect from the James Webb Space Telescope?
- A excellent value for money
- B more questions to be raised
- C enhanced pictures of space
- D proof of scientific theories

111 What does the passage say about comets?
- A Locating them can be a complex process.
- B They should be more thoroughly analyzed.
- C They may yield extremely important data.
- D Astronomers should pay them more attention.

112 How did astronomers come across the new comet?
- A during an experiment
- B after a conscious effort
- C with a special technique
- D by a stroke of luck

113 What are satellites helping public health authorities with?
- A warning people about local diseases
- B analyzing data from specific regions
- C predicting the frequency of storms
- D containing outbreaks of diseases

Not all discoveries made in space are about space itself, however, and one of the most important has been the use of satellite data to provide information on natural disasters and diseases. Advanced modelling using the Copernicus satellites can now act as early-warning systems for the spread of diseases such as malaria, enabling public health authorities to take preventative measures to combat specific instances and manage high-risk regions. It is yet another item on the ever-growing list of exciting developments brought about by this new phase in space research.

114 What does the author imply about space research?

  A Wider society does not reap the benefits of it.
  B Most people underestimate the importance of it.
  C Scientists have developed a renewed interest in it.
  D There isn't sufficient funding for it.

This passage is about hot air balloons.

When the first hot air balloon rose into the skies above Paris in 1783, one observer was fascinated by the spectacle unfolding before his eyes. That person was none other than Benjamin Franklin, one of the founding fathers of the USA, who was in Paris in his capacity as representative for the USA negotiating a treaty with French leaders. Franklin documented the flight and became intrigued by the ideas of aviation, predicting that air travel would soon become commonplace.

Soon after Franklin's return to the USA, Frenchman Jean Pierre Francois Blanchard, Europe's leading 'aeronaut' as the pilots were known, arrived in Philadelphia to demonstrate the hot air balloon. 'Balloon mania' had spread rapidly in Europe, and the Americans were keen to see what all the fuss was about. The first flight took place in January 1793 with Blanchard at the helm, and the forty-five-minute flight was a resounding success to all those who had gathered to watch, including President George Washington. Like Franklin and many of his contemporaries, Washington was an ardent supporter of technological innovation, and, after having witnessed the balloon flight, he was convinced that air travel would soon **take over** from sea travel between the Americas and Europe.

Further use and development of balloons as transportation in the USA were largely influenced by the interplay between commerce and conflict. During the late 19th Century, American inventor Thaddeus Lowe sought funding from Abraham Lincoln to develop his hot air balloons because he was convinced that they could contribute to winning the Civil War. Balloons were also used by the American military for surveillance and research purposes in the mid-20th century, the result of a Federal program that funded the construction of the modern, nylon-fabricated hot air balloon that used propane fuel.

115 What is the main purpose of the passage?
- A to discuss the inventors of hot air balloons
- B to explain the American connection to hot air balloons
- C to describe the technical aspects of the hot air balloon.
- D to give reasons why ballooning became popular

116 What was Benjamin Franklin's assessment of hot air balloon transport?
- A It needed further research.
- B It would never catch on.
- C It had limited potential.
- D It would become mainstream.

117 Why did a French aeronaut go to the USA in 1793?
- A to raise money from investors
- B to get support from the President
- C to encourage public interest
- D to satisfy people's curiosity

118 In the last sentence of paragraph 2, what word could best replace **take over**?
- A surpass
- B overlook
- C undermine
- D suppress

119 What was largely responsible for balloon development in the USA?
- A individual innovation
- B government investment
- C private finance
- D overseas collaboration

The company behind the invention of the modern hot air balloon was Raven Industries, set up by Ed Yost and his engineers, with help from an investor. They worked for some time on developing a prototype that was safe to fly, and, in 1960, Ed Yost became the first person to make a successful flight in a modern hot air balloon.

Over the following years Yost and his colleagues went on to set all manner of ballooning records related to distance and altitude. Raven Industries began to sell balloons commercially in the 1960s and launched a new recreational pastime that grew rapidly in popularity. Today there are approximately ten-thousand hot air balloon pilots worldwide, and remarkably, when compared to transport in general, the design of the hot air balloon remains largely unchanged from the original.

120 What is unique about hot air balloons as a form of transport?

- **A** The number of people that can fly them.
- **B** How long the initial design lasted.
- **C** They were most popular during the 1960s.
- **D** Only one company manufactures them.

Reading ECPE

Test 5

Reading ECPE

51 Climate change is _____ many individuals don't think that they can make any difference with their actions.

- A so large a problem that
- B as large a problem then
- C a too large problem so
- D such a large problem for

52 They wouldn't accept him back into the college, _____ begged them to.

- A even if he
- B as though he
- C he might have
- D while he has

53 Please take what you can because I'd _____ that food go to waste.

- A hate having
- B have hated
- C be hating
- D hate to have

54 Let's throw Gary a party for his birthday, but _____ until the day so it's a surprise.

- A keep it to him
- B keep it off
- C keep from him
- D keep it from him

55 I think Nick is _____ quitting the course as he's so stressed about the coursework.

- A bound to be
- B on the verge of
- C likely to have
- D about to be

56 The sales ideas were _____ because the company didn't have the budget to implement them

- A out to rule
- B ruled without
- C ruled out
- D out ruled

57 Public transportation in this city would improve no end _____ more funding.

- A had it been received
- B when it will receive
- C were it to receive
- D if it might receive

58 My parents let me out in the evening alone _____ back before 10:00pm.

- A so long as I'm
- B provided being
- C even if I get
- D in the event I go

59 Zara only found out that she _____ to present her report to the sales team a day before.

- **A** will be due
- **B** is due
- **C** was due
- **D** had due

60 Everybody in the class _____ their preparatory notes with their presentations.

- **A** was handing in
- **B** was made to hand in
- **C** was made hand in
- **D** was made handing in

61 King Autos are offering free test drives today to _____ with the new car stock that's just arrived.

- **A** encourage people to interact
- **B** be encouraging people interact
- **C** encourage to interact people
- **D** encouraging people interact

62 The actor's performance was so gripping that the audience _____ even the slightest sound.

- **A** to dare to make
- **B** dare not to make
- **C** didn't dare make
- **D** not dare making

63 The police are questioning somebody for jewel theft, but _____ to release the name to the press yet.

- **A** they are without liberty
- **B** they cannot in liberty
- **C** they are not at liberty
- **D** they do not have liberty

64 I didn't think much of the food at the restaurant, but _____ a nice atmosphere.

- **A** the place was having
- **B** the place did have
- **C** did the place have
- **D** hadn't the place

65 David stood tall _____ scare the large dog away, but it just turned and wandered off.

- **A** so as for
- **B** such that he
- **C** as if to
- **D** in so much to

66 If only _____ too hard yesterday, I might not have gotten injured.

- **A** I hadn't trained
- **B** I wasn't to train
- **C** I didn't train
- **D** I haven't been training

This passage is about telescopes.

For amateur astronomers, choosing a telescope can be a real **67)**_____ because the options seem endless. Trying to figure out those that meet your requirements is **68)**_____, and many people are put off at the mere **69)**_____.
On more than one occasion, telescope companies have **70)**_____ consumers for their inability to help prospective buyers understand their product ranges and the relative merits and demerits of each model. **71)**_____ consumers are willing to do the research to find the right model is understandably limited.

Nonetheless, there are some golden rules worth considering. First and foremost, don't just **72)**_____ the cheap products, as these are perfectly adequate in rural areas where the sky is usually **73)**_____ at night, making it highly likely that you'll get good results even with basic equipment.

However, the situation is far trickier in urban environments that have severe light pollution. To **74)**_____ anything other than planets, you should invest in a light-pollution filter, as these simple gadgets can achieve **75)**_____ with minimal spending. Also, bear in mind that buying an expensive telescope will have a **76)**_____ effect on your ability to see anything in great detail in cities compared to in the countryside.

67	A discomfort		C inquiry	
	B ordeal		D contradiction	
68	A an irrational chore		C a desperate plan	
	B a formidable task		D an impulsive quest	
69	A prospect		C aspiration	
	B outlook		D purpose	
70	A gone overboard with		C lost sight of	
	B stood their ground with		D come under fire from	
71	A The extent to which		C By any chance	
	B At one time or another		D In no uncertain terms	
72	A narrow down		C rule out	
	B put aside		D press on	
73	A dim		C secluded	
	B pitch-dark		D flawless	
74	A see eye to eye with		C stand a chance of seeing	
	B keep your eyes open for		D be on the same wavelength as	
75	A a faraway look		C the means to an end	
	B a stroke of luck		D the desired result	
76	A negligible		C dubious	
	B detrimental		D indifferent	

67	A	B	C	D		68	A	B	C	D		69	A	B	C	D		70	A	B	C	D
71	A	B	C	D		72	A	B	C	D		73	A	B	C	D		74	A	B	C	D
75	A	B	C	D		76	A	B	C	D												

This passage is about Josephine Baker.

The life of Josephine Baker is a 77)_____ tale that wouldn't look out of place in a work of fiction. Born into poverty in St Louis in the USA, Josephine's childhood paints a 78)_____ picture of the hardships endured by black females in early 20th-century America. Put to work from the age of eight as a live-in domestic helper, 79)_____ by employees and married off in her early teens, Josephine set her sights on a better existence away from the desperate world of her youth.

Drawn to the 80)_____ of the entertainment world, she left for New York after gaining a position dancing with a touring production, and before long she found herself in Paris, where she 81)_____ on the dance scene, something that would change her life beyond her 82)_____. Her unusual style of dancing, and Josephine herself, were 83)_____ by the French, and the nation adopted her as one of their most beloved celebrities.

She didn't confine herself to the realm of entertainment, however. During the Second World War, she 84)_____ to serve her adopted country, for which she was awarded France's most distinguished medal for bravery, and during visits to the USA she campaigned against racial 85)_____, which was prevalent at the time in America and 86)_____ the progressive attitudes in France.

| 77 | A | breath of fresh air | C | rags to riches |
| | B | blow your mind | D | doom and gloom |

| 78 | A | grim | C | frantic |
| | B | hollow | D | persistent |

| 79 | A | detached | C | condemned |
| | B | mistreated | D | wretched |

| 80 | A | lure | C | deception |
| | B | glow | D | vanity |

| 81 | A | span around | C | held out hope |
| | B | went with the flow | D | made a splash |

| 82 | A | own accord | C | wildest dreams |
| | B | bottom line | D | humble opinion |

| 83 | A | channeled | C | indulged |
| | B | flourished | D | embraced |

| 84 | A | leant on | C | set out |
| | B | stepped up | D | caught on |

| 85 | A | recognition | C | segregation |
| | B | provocation | D | withdrawal |

| 86 | A | far removed from | C | the tail end of |
| | B | bound up with | D | along the lines of |

87 Jess is so pleased that she's _____ a job in marine conservation.

A considered
B planted
C landed
D lead

88 Remember to _____ so you can prepare for any unforeseen circumstances.

A think ahead
B open up
C own up
D come round

89 After much _____, they decided to sell their house and move to the city.

A hesitation
B conversion
C occupation
D elimination

90 Some new-born animals _____ about a bit before they can walk confidently.

A shudder
B stagger
C saddle
D squander

91 This program runs for six _____ weeks across the summer.

A consecutive
B compulsive
C compatible
D credible

92 The new taxes will be a _____ to single people, who will be affected far more than families.

A brick
B bite
C blow
D block

93 The actor _____ claimed that their success was down to the other cast members and crew.

A modestly
B visibly
C candidly
D tolerantly

94 Even successful sports stars have to _____ losing sometimes.

A come to terms with
B steer clear of
C fall short of
D catch sight of

95 Getting courses approved by a well-known college adds to their _____.

- A attachment
- B intuition
- C backing
- D credibility

96 Remodelling the building at this stage of the project will _____ significant costs.

- A invite
- B settle
- C quote
- D incur

97 Juliana Garcia is one of the most influential designers on the fashion _____ at the moment.

- A route
- B track
- C circuit
- D domain

98 Make sure that you _____ in the house while I go shopping.

- A stay put
- B come apart
- C give way
- D let go

99 Speaking calmly and confidently can be difficult when you're under the _____ of the media.

- A peek
- B glare
- C flash
- D squint

100 Anderson College _____ to provide students with the best professional training.

- A bids
- B establishes
- C strives
- D implies

101 Professor Granger's analyses _____ so clearly in her lectures.

- A come out
- B come across
- C come by
- D come along

102 The _____ eye color in our family is brown.

- A forceful
- B imperial
- C dominant
- D assertive

This passage is about geysers.

Geysers are an extremely rare geological occurrence due to the highly specific conditions required for their formation, namely underground rocks at high temperatures, underground water and cracks in the Earth's crust to allow this water access to the surface. They are similar to hot springs, with one notable difference, which is that rather than the water appearing on the Earth's surface by bubbling up in pools, geysers spurt plumes of steam and water into the air, sometimes to breath-taking heights.

The most famous geyser, Old Faithful, located in the southern part of Yellowstone National Park, Wyoming, **embodies** this spectacle perfectly, and on any given day of the week, groups of tourists gather, cameras at the ready, waiting to gasp as it spews columns of water and steam over 375 feet into the sky. The tourists may not be the only people there however, as this geyser is one of the most thoroughly observed by scientists. Given that its name comes from the fact that its eruptions are regular, it is far better placed for study than others that are less reliable and therefore provide less data.

Old Faithful is indeed a sight to behold and Yellowstone National Park is one of the few locations in the world to observe such a phenomenon. In fact, outside of the park, only four other countries are home to geysers: Russia, New Zealand, Chile and Iceland (the word 'geyser' originates from the Icelandic word meaning 'to gush'). Relatively little is known about the Valley of Geysers in Russia as access to this remote location prevents adequate investigation, and in the USA scientists are restricted in their access to geysers because of the protected status of Yellowstone as a National Park. In contrast, geologists have been allowed more access to El Tatio Geyser Field in The Atacama Desert in Chile, and as a result this is proving to be an exciting research site.

103 What is the main purpose of the passage?
  A to explore the attraction of geysers
  B to outline scientific research on geysers
  C to highlight the scarcity of geysers
  D to explain how geysers are formed

104 What is true about geysers?
  A They are unstable.
  B They are graceful.
  C They are innumerable.
  D They are scarce.

105 In the first sentence of the second paragraph, what word could best replace **embodies**?
  A produces
  B defines
  C interprets
  D demonstrates

106 What does the passage say about Old Faithful?
  A Its behavior justifies research.
  B It is in a beautiful location.
  C It attracts admirers from far away.
  D It is highly unpredictable.

107 According to the author, why do geologists enjoy working in El Tatio?
  A The geysers' behavior is unusual.
  B They can do more in-depth research.
  C Their results have been clearer.
  D They have higher status in Chile.

Geysers can provide insights into other areas of interest to geologists such as volcanic eruptions and the influence of climate change or events on the Earth's geology. An example of this occurred in 2002 when an earthquake in Alaska, which, according to scientists working in Yellowstone National Park over 1,200 miles away, had a profound and almost immediate impact on the geysers there. Within a few hours, new geysers had formed and the frequency of eruptions in the existing geysers started to change. All this highlights how useful geysers are for learning about the Earth's underground natural processes.

108 How did an earthquake in Alaska effect geysers in Yellowstone National Park?

- **A** They started to erupt more frequently.
- **B** Their depth increased significantly.
- **C** There was a range of reactions.
- **D** Their eruptions increased in intensity.

103	A	B	C	D
107	A	B	C	D

104	A	B	C	D
108	A	B	C	D

105	A	B	C	D

106	A	B	C	D

This passage is about introverts.

The modern world clearly values extroverts more than introverts, and nowhere is this attitude more prevalent than in the USA. Introverts are constantly encouraged to open up and engage more with others, be it at school, in the workplace or in their social lives, whereas extroverts are presented as a model that we should all aim for. But is there actually any evidence to support this claim that a world full of extroverts is the ideal? In recent years, large bodies of research have concluded that this view is indeed misguided, and, in light of this research, it has been suggested that the world should take a fresh look at introverts from a more positive perspective.

First of all, it is important to understand from where this admiration of extroverts originated. The psychologist Carl Jung coined the term 'extrovert' in the 1920s, and it gradually gained ground among other psychologists until it became a social standard to aspire to during the mid-to-late 20th Century. However, when examined in detail, many of the benefits associated with extroverts seem quite ridiculous. Take, for example, the belief that extroverts make good leaders. If we assume that strong leadership is based on qualities such as thoughtfulness, reflection and the ability to assess multiple views, it **stands to reason** that introverts are more likely to perform better than extroverts, who can be impulsive, poor listeners and crave attention.

Another idea that has been disputed is that groupwork is the best route to creativity. An example of how much support this idea has received can be seen in certain American high schools and workplaces, where furniture placement is intended to help people collaborate on tasks, thereby encouraging people to be more extrovert. This is seen as an improvement on previous practices whereby school children and employees had single desks and often worked on tasks individually. Again, studies show that groupwork, especially brainstorming as a form of creativity, is deeply

109 What is the main purpose of the passage?
- A to revise an old theory
- B to challenge a common view
- C to encourage creative thinking
- D to highlight a need for change

110 What does the passage say about leadership?
- A Extroverts are ill-suited to it.
- B Very few people excel at it.
- C Introverts do not respond well to it.
- D Specific skills are required for it.

111 In the last sentence of the second paragraph, what words could best replace **it stands to reason**?
- A the bottom line is
- B it comes to light
- C you would suppose
- D it is beyond dispute

112 What point does the author make about people working together in groups?
- A It produces ideas of superior quality.
- B It profoundly influences room design.
- C It functions well in the workplace.
- D Its value is upheld by research.

113 According to the passage, what has sustained society's views on introverts?
- A personal stories
- B dated reports
- C incorrect studies
- D unproven opinions

flawed, and that working alone is far more likely to result in creativity. And again, it could be argued that these conclusions are common sense if we consider the number of artists, inventors and entrepreneurs who worked in solitary environments and yet made huge contributions to knowledge, technology and society.

It is clear that our understanding of these two personality types has long been based on assumptions rather than evidence, and that an overdue re-evaluation is taking place. Whether this will bring lasting change to the way half the population is judged, we will have to wait and see.

114 What can be concluded about introverts?
- **A** They make highly successful leaders.
- **B** They are naturally creative people.
- **C** Their approach to work is not respected.
- **D** They have been unfairly criticized.

This passage is about baseball.

Baseball is the national sport of the USA, and a huge money-making business with individual teams making in the region of $300 million in revenue annually. However, according to sports historians, its origin story, believed by many, ¡is actually a fallacy.

It was a long-held common belief that baseball was invented by an army general, Abner Doubleday, in 1839. This understanding **hailed** from the result of the Mills Commission, an investigation undertaken in the early 1900s to ascertain baseball's true origins. The study aimed to clear a bone of contention concerning whether the game was a true US invention or was adapted from an earlier game, called rounders, played by the British and Irish.

After the commission appealed to the public for information regarding the origin of baseball, a response came in from an Abner Graves, who claimed to have been in attendance at the very first baseball game, where his friend, Doubleday, had established the rules. While the commission requested further evidence, this wasn't forthcoming, with Graves stating that, since 70 years had passed since that first game, the players had all since passed away, as had Doubleday himself. Despite this, the commission still found in favor of Graves' claim.

While this may be sufficiently suspicious for the more cynical among us, there are further facts that could lead us to consider Graves' assertion to be dubious. Firstly, in 1839 Graves was only five-years old, and his declaration to the commission was made around 70 years later. Therefore, it's possible that his memory was inaccurate. Furthermore, in an interview with a local newspaper shortly after the commission's findings, Graves' version of events was inconsistent with his earlier statements to the commission. Finally, during his lifetime, Doubleday himself never made claim to the invention of baseball.

Despite all this, the judgement that Doubleday invented the game has never been formally overturned, and to this day the Doubleday myth, for some, is a reality, leaving the real origin story of baseball a mystery.

115 What is the main purpose of the passage?
- A to explain the historical contexts of baseball
- B to argue that baseball has British origins
- C to outline a common misconception in baseball
- D to describe where the term baseball originated

116 In the second sentence of paragraph 2, which words could replace **hailed**?
- A sprung
- B plunged
- C broke
- D caught

117 Why was the Mills Commission started?
- A to originate a concept
- B to dispel a myth
- C to reinforce a theory
- D to settle a dispute

118 What did Abner Graves fail to provide?
- A interviews
- B eyewitnesses
- C game rules
- D precise details

119 What does the writer allude to in paragraph 4?
- A that most people are wary of Graves' claims
- B that Graves acted deceitfully to the commission
- C that inconsistencies were hidden at the time
- D that Graves' version of events may be flawed

120 What does the passage say about Graves' claims?

- **A** They encouraged patriotism.
- **B** They were originally controversial.
- **C** They aren't widely believed anymore.
- **D** They distract from the truth.

Reading ECPE
Test 6

51. Mr Davies is _____ you'll find in this school.
   A as dedicated teacher which
   B as dedicated a teacher as
   C a dedicated teacher as
   D the dedicated teacher as

52. The condo is great except for the noise of the planes from the nearby airport that _____ at night.
   A keeps us to up
   B keeps us up
   C keeps up us
   D keeps with us

53. Just give the admissions office a call and we'll _____ with your application.
   A start rolling the ball
   B roll the ball out
   C ball out and roll
   D get the ball rolling

54. If students have issues with classes, they must go to the manager, _____ responsibilities is to review complaints.
   A of whom has
   B one of whose
   C which one of
   D who has one of

55. I can see Jean's car still parked outside, so she _____ far.
   A couldn't be going
   B couldn't have been going
   C couldn't have gone
   D couldn't be gone

56. There was thick ice on that lake in the old days, but, now that it doesn't freeze over, kids can't skate on it _____.
   A like we were used to
   B since we used to
   C as we used to do
   D how we used it

57. I'd definitely relocate _____ the fact that my family are all nearby.
   A if it were not for
   B were not it for
   C if not it was
   D not that it was for

58. No matter _____, you'll never manage to get that old truck working again.
   A to try how hard
   B trying how hard
   C as you try hard
   D how hard you try

59 Unfortunately, the city caught _____ of the storm and there was considerable damage done.

   A the tail end
   B the tail's end
   C a tailing end
   D a tail end

60 _____ children should be disciplined at a young age is a matter for their parents to decide.

   A Whatever for
   B Whenever that
   C Whereby and when
   D Whether or not

61 James was far from proficient at French, _____ have any inclination to improve.

   A nor did he
   B neither he did
   C he neither nor
   D nor he was

62 You _____ the book to truly appreciate the movie version.

   A are to have read
   B have had read
   C have to have read
   D all having to read

63 _____, the average person is slightly taller when they wake up than when they go to bed.

   A Might it seem strange however
   B However strange it might seem
   C However it might seem strange
   D It might seem strange however

64 You'll just have to _____ less free time and focus on the advantages of this promotion.

   A reconcile you to have
   B reconcile your to having
   C reconcile yourself to having
   D reconcile you with having

65 They are going to install _____ machine in the foyer of the building.

   A a new water
   B new waters
   C some new waters
   D new water

66 We would have found out about the travel disruption downtown _____ the news earlier.

   A if we were tuned in
   B were we had tuned into
   C had we tuned into
   D had we to tune into

This passage is about language development.

Anyone who has tried to acquire a second language as an adult will tell you that it can be tricky to even **67)**_____ the basics. However, while as adults we may struggle with learning the speech and grammar of another tongue, young children seem to be able to pick this **68)**_____ ability up with significantly less exertion, making the **69)**_____ that perhaps, where possible, children should be raised bilingually.

Ideally this should commence at birth, as a baby's ability to **70)**_____ between different sounds in languages is an **71)**_____ that is lost at just one year old, when they can no longer **72)**_____ a distinction between sounds in languages they haven't been exposed to. Admittedly, there is some concern that children raised bilingually may **73)**_____ in learning vocabulary, but **74)**_____ is still out on whether this is correct, with research indicating that their combined vocabulary of both languages is equal or greater than that of their monolingual peers. Additionally, many cognitive advantages can be **75)**_____ from being raised bilingually, including enhanced problem-solving skills. So, for anyone who wants to give their children a linguistic advantage, start sooner rather than later, so they don't **76)**_____!

| 67 | A | snatch | C | grasp |
| | B | carve | D | embrace |

| 68 | A | explosive | C | exclusive |
| | B | elusive | D | elated |

| 69 | A | certainty | C | challenge |
| | B | command | D | case |

| 70 | A | disassociate | C | disconcert |
| | B | disclose | D | discriminate |

| 71 | A | attribute | C | indication |
| | B | empathy | D | orientation |

| 72 | A | paint | C | mark |
| | B | outline | D | draw |

| 73 | A | fall behind | C | fall off |
| | B | fall under | D | fall back |

| 74 | A | the jury | C | the trial |
| | B | the defendant | D | the court |

| 75 | A | evolved | C | derived |
| | B | traced | D | extracted |

| 76 | A | get in the same boat | C | rock the boat |
| | B | miss the boat | D | push the boat out |

Part 2 | Multiple-choice Cloze | Test 6

This passage is about bears.

Imagine you're strolling through the woods one afternoon when suddenly you 77)_____ a bear on the track ahead. If you believe all the media reports about bears, you're in some serious trouble and had better 78)_____ and shin up the nearest tree before you're 79)_____. Yet, as with most things reported in the media nowadays, the reactions to occurrences of bear attacks are completely out of 80)_____ given that bear attacks on humans in North America are extremely 81)_____.

As wildlife biologists frequently remind us, bear behavior is widely misunderstood; most people characterize it in terms of their own fear. Bears are highly intelligent, social animals that form 82)_____ relationships with followers and leaders, and happily share resources. For some 83)_____ reason, the media and popular culture have 84)_____ them as ferocious animals always ready to attack, whereas in reality this could not be further from the truth. Whilst it is worth 85)_____ whenever you're out walking in mountains, which are known bear habitats, 86)_____ you won't even spot a bear let alone be attacked by one.

| 77 | A | come about | C | stumble across |
| | B | head off | D | run around |

| 78 | A | make a run for it | C | pull your weight |
| | B | fear the worst | D | get a move on |

| 79 | A | shaken up | C | kicked off |
| | B | torn apart | D | held back |

| 80 | A | line | C | season |
| | B | proportion | D | touch |

| 81 | A | off the beaten track | C | touch and go |
| | B | far removed | D | few and far between |

| 82 | A | predominant | C | hierarchical |
| | B | superior | D | parallel |

| 83 | A | inexplicable | C | thoughtless |
| | B | disillusioned | D | contradictory |

| 84 | A | portrayed | C | targeted |
| | B | prescribed | D | stamped |

| 85 | A | keeping your temper | C | being on your guard |
| | B | going through the motions | D | gaining the upper hand |

| 86 | A | in perspective | C | on principle |
| | B | for the best | D | in all likelihood |

87 When it came to sentencing the defendant, the judge showed no _____.

- A mercy
- B dignity
- C clarity
- D charisma

88 The birth of their daughter was _____ with joy by the whole family.

- A stirred
- B retrieved
- C marked
- D greeted

89 People with _____ lifestyles are most at risk of obesity and heart disease.

- A sedentary
- B versatile
- C pathetic
- D redundant

90 Johan says his lack of computer skills is _____.

- A handing him down
- B tipping him off
- C holding him back
- D tracking him down

91 The report _____ mentioned the financial difficulties the company has faced, focusing on more positive aspects instead.

- A abruptly
- B wholly
- C scarcely
- D roughly

92 _____, the tiger cubs survived until adulthood.

- A As it stands
- B Against all the odds
- C Not in the least
- D In all probability

93 The painting sold for over $1 million before it was discovered that it was a _____.

- A hoax
- B fake
- C scam
- D mirror

94 Athletes have to _____ a high level of performance to win many competitions.

- A sustain
- B urge
- C differentiate
- D commit

95 Mountain climbers must take great care because they are always _____ the weather.

A at the hands of
B at the mercy of
C in the face of
D in the process of

96 The mayor's office has _____ on funding for the arts this year.

A fallen back
B stirred up
C sealed off
D cut back

97 Last night's _____ caused considerable damage to the roofs of many cars.

A drizzle
B coral
C dew
D hail

98 When questioned, the boys' stories _____ one another.

A contradicted
B blocked
C exclaimed
D disqualified

99 At Hailsford College we believe there is no _____ to success, and our impressive alumni list proves this.

A brake
B rail
C wall
D bar

100 This hotel suite is one of our most _____, with a jacuzzi and a roof terrace overlooking the city.

A obscene
B lavish
C dazed
D finite

101 Make sure that you _____ the contract before sending it to the client.

A strike
B amend
C equate
D vow

102 Finding _____ can be the most difficult part of writing a novel.

A imitation
B inspiration
C composition
D conviction

Reading ECPE

This passage is about uncertainty.

You never know what the future holds, and while individuals usually manage to get on with things without worrying about what is beyond their control, thinking about all the eventualities is one of the paramount concerns for businesses. In the world of work, uncertainty is concerned with the inability to predict or influence events that may impact negatively on the business. This shouldn't be confused with the term 'risk', which, while similar in meaning, can be assessed, and analyzed in ways that uncertainty can't be, therefore giving businesses the luxury of potentially mitigating any negative consequences. This kind of mitigation is simply not a facet of uncertainty, which is something that can spring from nowhere.

This is not to state that nothing can be done about uncertainty, but usually it's a reactive activity rather than something premeditated. One of the most essential actions businesses can take when encountering a situation of uncertainty is to face it. When some event beyond their control rears its ugly head, rather than shy away from it managers need to roll their sleeves up and prioritize contingency plans, with ideas of what to do in the short and medium term to limit any damage. For example, if trade problems between two countries severely affect a company's exports, it's critical to work on efforts to minimize this disruption. It's not easy of course, and additional business lines around the core of the business may need to be cut adrift, but the most important goal is survival in these circumstances.

Another way that uncertainty can tear through a business is if the company places all its eggs in one basket, or, to put it more simply, has a very narrow service or product offering. Uncertainty can affect any part of a business, ranging from shortages of materials to regional difficulties or whole-industry breakdown, so, where possible, diversification in a company's offerings can be a welcome safety belt to combat the effects of uncertainty.

103 What is the main purpose of the passage?
  A to argue why uncertainty is an intrinsic part of business
  B to outline why businesses need to face uncertainty
  C to describe how businesses can cope with uncertainty
  D to highlight how uncertainty can affect businesses

104 What does the writer say about risk?
  A it is optional
  B it is tangible
  C it is beneficial
  D it is unexpected

105 What advice for businesses does the writer give in paragraph 2?
  A to focus on maintaining the central offering
  B to look at how products can be diversified
  C to make new plans in order to change the core product
  D to make sure everyone is working hard to fix problems

106 What should businesses do to avoid materials shortages?
  A work with many regions
  B have a back-up plan
  C change suppliers
  D broaden their products

107 In paragraph 4, sentence 2, which word could replace **outside the box**?
  A impulsively
  B ethically
  C proactively
  D imaginatively

Take, for example, how hard a shoe manufacturer that only works with leather shoes would be hit by a ban on leather compared to a similar business that uses a wider range of materials.

An additional point to think about in terms of dealing with uncertainty is ensuring that a company can make flexible adjustments during a time of crisis. One obvious example of this is how some companies survived during the Covid-19 pandemic by thinking **outside the box**. While people weren't spending money on traditional businesses during the global pandemic, some of the more inventive minds of business shifted their production to providing medical equipment or to making payments fully contactless where possible.

Lastly, during uncertain times communication and transparency when communicating with its employees is essential for any business. From bottom to top, everyone in a company is worried about uncertainty in their work, and employees need to understand the security of their jobs as much as possible. Businesses should make sure that they update workers constantly about the company's financial situation and plans to move forward, so that they are invested and pull together to come out of the tough times.

108 Why should employees be made aware of uncertainty?

- **A** to help them to plan for their own futures
- **B** to create a feeling of care towards the company's future
- **C** to let them know that tough times are ahead
- **D** to ensure that they work harder to pull through

103	A	B	C	D
107	A	B	C	D

104	A	B	C	D
108	A	B	C	D

105	A	B	C	D

106	A	B	C	D

This passage is about Hollywood.

In our collective minds, the Californian neighborhood of Hollywood is so much more than just a physical location. It's also synonymous with the glitz and glamour of the silver screen, and a dream destination for anyone who wishes to make a name for themselves on the big screen. What is widely considered to be the world's oldest movie industry was established there, but little over a century ago the area was a far cry from its current appearance.

In the late 1800s, the locality was an agricultural community, with the majority of residents being four-legged rather than studio bosses and superstars. Modern 'Hollywood' **came into being** in the early 1900s, when a developer bought the farmland to construct a high-class neighborhood and hotel in addition to incorporating its now-famous name.

At the same time, on the east coast of the USA, the very first movies were being made by inventor Thomas Edison, who had patented the moving-image process. This made it costly or dangerous for other moviemakers to work as they had to either pay expensive fees to Edison or use equipment illicitly in the hope of not getting caught. While many people believe this was responsible for the movie industry's origins in west coast Hollywood, it seems to be far from the only explanation.

In fact, many entrepreneurs realized that California was ideal for moviemaking, thanks to its large open spaces, sparse rainfall, comparatively cheap land and, fundamentally, unlike the east coast, its terrain. It was the perfect backdrop for Westerns, the mainstream genre of the era, highlighting the pioneering spirit of the time. Hollywood was further **heralded** as a movie epicentre when director D.W. Griffiths ventured out to different areas in California to make the first Hollywood movie, 'In Old California'.

By the late 1910s, the principal movie studios had established themselves in Hollywood, and went from strength to strength, even during the Great Depression of the 1930s.

109 What is the main purpose of the passage?
- A to explain the advantages of Hollywood
- B to outline the origins of Hollywood
- C to describe the problems of early moviemaking
- D to explore how moviemaking started in the USA

110 In the second line of paragraph 2, which word can best replace **came into being**?
- A came to light
- B came to mind
- C came about
- D came along

111 With what did early moviemakers have problems?
- A intimidation
- B space
- C apparatus
- D rights

112 What was the best thing about the west coast?
- A Its climate
- B Its cost-effectiveness
- C Its landscape
- D Its pioneering spirit

113 In the second line of the fourth paragraph, which word can best replace **heralded**?
- A nominated
- B examined
- C deduced
- D signaled

It turns out that, even through times of desperate hardships, the escapism of the big screen is a big draw, which is also why the movie industry is commonly known as 'recession proof', something we can certainly believe if Hollywood is any indicator.

114 What does the writer say about the movie industry?

- **A** It has an unfair reputation.
- **B** It has consistently succeeded.
- **C** It's stronger during recessions.
- **D** It's strongest in Hollywood.

109	A	B	C	D
113	A	B	C	D

110	A	B	C	D
114	A	B	C	D

111	A	B	C	D

112	A	B	C	D

This passage is about the Bermuda Triangle.

A part of the far-reaching ocean where people mysteriously disappear no matter whether they fly or sail through it? It sounds the stuff of legends, doesn't it? However, some people contend that this kind of phenomena exists in what is known as the Bermuda Triangle.

The Bermuda Triangle is a vast, triangular area of the Atlantic Ocean that stretches from Florida to Bermuda via Puerto Rico, and has become known as a much more than just another stretch of sea. The story of the Bermuda Triangle was born the 1950s, when people started noting mysterious disappearances of both ships and planes in the area. It is a moniker so well-known that it also spawned an international hit for irrepressible crooner Barry Manilow in the 1980s.

For many people, the Bermuda Triangle is simply an urban legend, something that sparks the imagination of conspiracy theorists and **sensationalists** worldwide. This perspective is understandable when we look at some of the extraordinary theories that have been expounded on the mystery of the region, theories that, at their most outlandish, include technology from the lost city of Atlantis and a time warp that sucks people into another dimension.

While these ideas might be amusing to entertain, for the majority of people they just aren't credible explanations for the disappearances in the area. This is not to say that there haven't been theories that have held water, especially ones revolving around environmental phenomena such as the changes in the Gulf Stream, an ocean current that can bring strong and sudden weather changes, or simply the number of hurricanes present in that area. Yet, whether we need to explore any more theories is truly open to debate.

115 What is the main purpose of the passage?
- A to explain what the mystery of the Bermuda Triangle is about
- B to explore the history surrounding the Bermuda Triangle
- C to discuss whether the Bermuda Triangle is special or not
- D to outline the scientific explanation of the Bermuda Triangle

116 Why is the name of the Bermuda Triangle famous?
- A because of a song
- B because of its geography
- C because of a shipwreck
- D because of its reputation

117 In paragraph 3, line 1, which word could best replace **sensationalists**?
- A loudmouths
- B gossips
- C bigots
- D tricksters

118 In paragraph 5, sentence 1, which term could replace the phrase **with a pinch of salt**?
- A lightly
- B suspiciously
- C seriously
- D bluntly

119 What are the chances of crashing in the Bermuda Triangle?
- A too difficult to evaluate accurately
- B much higher than elsewhere
- C slightly higher than elsewhere
- D the same as anywhere else

Even these days on the internet it's no trouble at all to come across many a snappy article or soundbite video concerning the truth of the Bermuda Triangle being ´finally revealed´, but the smart reader would do well to take these **with a pinch of salt**. The evidence seems to suggest that the whole commotion around the Bermuda Triangle was built on half-truths and wild imaginations, and that claims of even slightly more peril in this part of the ocean compared to others are in fact dubious. This is supported by insurers Lloyds of London, who don't put a risk premium on the Bermuda Triangle at all, stating that the region has as much a chance of experiencing a crash or sinking than any other ocean setting. So, if you're thinking of sailing the seven seas any time soon, put your worries into navigating the truly perilous patches of sea, like Cape Horn, and sit back and enjoy the cruising around Bermuda!

120 Which word best describes the writer's view on the subject?

- **A** amused
- **B** cynical
- **C** puzzled
- **D** worried

115	A	B	C	D
119	A	B	C	D

116	A	B	C	D
120	A	B	C	D

117	A	B	C	D

118	A	B	C	D

Reading ECPE
Test 7

51 When Lucy got to the airport, she _____ idea how to get to her hotel.

- **A** only knew the slightest
- **B** wasn't the slightest
- **C** just knew the slightest
- **D** didn't have the slightest

52 It's still in doubt _____ for a second term.

- **A** when the President is running
- **B** if the President is run
- **C** that the President is to run
- **D** whether the President will run

53 Many people enjoy travelling, but few _____ give up their jobs and journey around the world.

- **A** go too far that
- **B** go so far as to
- **C** go that far so to
- **D** go as far for to

54 The first KC Jones movie was somewhat predictable, but _____ amazing action scenes.

- **A** it had had some
- **B** did it have some
- **C** it did have some
- **D** some it did have

55 The cafeteria is closed at the moment because the college is _____.

- **A** to be refurbished it
- **B** being refurbished it
- **C** has it refurbished
- **D** having it refurbished

56 _____ when the Brooklyn Bears star player was taken off with an injury.

- **A** Hardly started had the game
- **B** Hardly had the game started
- **C** Had the game hardly started
- **D** Had hardly the game started

57 It's quite _____ not to call and let us know they'd be late.

- **A** to unlike
- **B** unlike of them
- **C** unlike them
- **D** they're unlike

58 When Pete was training for track and field at college, he _____ by the coach for his arrogant attitude.

- **A** was constantly being yelled at
- **B** has constantly been yelled at
- **C** had been constantly yelling at
- **D** constantly was to be yelling at

59 My boss gave me a raise recently, and to _____ I also got the employee of the month award.

- A top of it all
- B top it all off
- C top off all
- D top it off all

60 Had Julia been in less of rush, she _____ her phone on the kitchen table.

- A wouldn't have been leaving
- B wouldn't have left
- C wouldn't be leaving
- D wouldn't leave

61 The report was so hard to understand that even after reading it twice I'm _____.

- A not the wisest
- B not much wisest
- C none the wiser
- D none to be wise

62 _____ book your trip with us, you'll get a personal travel advisor to help you with any queries.

- A You should choose to
- B When you choose that
- C Should you choose to
- D If you choose that

63 _____ in the house for the weekend while his parents were on vacation, Dean decided to have a party.

- A Having had been left
- B Having to have left
- C Having had left
- D Having been left

64 Harry and Lisa work well together, and _____ the other's positive traits.

- A each of them respects
- B they each respects
- C they respect each
- D each of they respect

65 The freeway is the only route into the city right now, so it _____ since about 6:00am this morning.

- A will be backed up
- B will be backing up
- C will have been backed up
- D will have backed up

66 _____ the scholarship program, some students wouldn't be able to afford the course.

- A If not it were for
- B Were it not for if
- C Had it not to be for
- D If it hadn't been for

This passage is about glaciers.

Of all the different types of scenery in North America, those that inspire the most **67)**_____ in people are glaciers, immense slow-moving sheets of ice that **68)**_____ out unique natural landscapes. Snow **69)**_____ glaciers when significant quantities accumulate into layers that build on one another and gradually turn into a mass of ice over many years.

To be classified as a glacier, this gigantic quantity of ice must be capable of movement. This **70)**_____ occurs when the compacted snow is over 150 feet in depth and its size and weight become susceptible to the **71)**_____ of gravity. Due to these factors, glaciers are only found in extremely mountainous areas, often at high altitude.

Glaciers move at variable speeds **72)**_____, and as they travel they scratch the surface of the Earth, **73)**_____ it as they go. This movement cannot be seen **74)**_____, but using a time-lapse camera and speeding up the video recording highlights this natural phenomenon clearly.

Sadly, glaciers are disappearing at an alarming rate, and a **75)**_____ of this is The Glacier National Park in Montana, which, according to scientists, **76)**_____ the majority of its glaciers in as little as fifteen years.

67	A	empathy	C	illusion	
	B	awe	D	harmony	
68	A	shape	C	carve	
	B	cast	D	drain	
69	A	binds	C	attaches	
	B	merges	D	forms	
70	A	invariably	C	intensely	
	B	allegedly	D	harshly	
71	A	concentration	C	severity	
	B	force	D	measurement	
72	A	downhill	C	fluidly	
	B	drifting	D	faraway	
73	A	undermining	C	peeling	
	B	crumbling	D	eroding	
74	A	eye to eye	C	in your mind's eye	
	B	in the blink of an eye	D	with the naked eye	
75	A	vicious cycle	C	sharp contrast	
	B	prime example	D	wild guess	
76	A	puts to one side	C	stands to lose	
	B	gives rise to	D	draws the line at	

This passage is about Air Force One.

The term 'Air Force One' technically 77)_____ any plane that holds the President, but most people use it to refer to the two identical Boeing 747 planes that are the President's habitual form of air transport. As you might imagine, there is 78)_____ in their construction, both in terms of the interior and exterior of the aircrafts. They each have three floors that include offices, bedrooms, kitchens and even a gym; every possible thing that might 79)_____ for the President and his team.

The qualities and behaviors of these presidential planes are highly unconventional in order to ensure the utmost safety in any 80)_____. For example, these planes always take off simultaneously and follow unusual flight 81)_____ in the air in order to 82)_____ the President's exact location.

The planes are also capable of refuelling mid-air, and are equipped with the latest technology to ensure that communications cannot be 83)_____, therefore being able to work as a command center if needed. In fact, these planes could be in the air 84)_____ if the President ever needed to run the country remotely. If that's not enough safety, 85)_____ Air Force One at all times is an additional aircraft, called the Doomsday plane, which is essentially an armor-plated nuclear bunker that can be used as a 86)_____ by the President.

77	A	denotes	C	exemplifies
	B	coincides	D	boasts

78	A	worthy of attention	C	no expense spared
	B	a force to be reckoned with	D	an unknown quantity

79	A	be an effort	C	derive comfort
	B	come in useful	D	let off steam

80	A	retreat	C	scenario
	B	patch	D	orientation

81	A	formations	C	instructions
	B	circuits	D	assemblies

82	A	filter	C	offset
	B	handle	D	obscure

83	A	succumbed	C	testified
	B	compromised	D	reconstructed

84	A	predominantly	C	conclusively
	B	strategically	D	indefinitely

85	A	in attendance	C	in the vicinity of
	B	at a loss	D	on the verge of

86	A	change of heart	C	turn for the worse
	B	last resort	D	strong support

77	A	B	C	D
81	A	B	C	D
85	A	B	C	D

78	A	B	C	D
82	A	B	C	D
86	A	B	C	D

79	A	B	C	D
83	A	B	C	D

80	A	B	C	D
84	A	B	C	D

87 The decision to raise rail ticket prices _____ outrage from many commuters.

- A recollected
- B pinpointed
- C sparked
- D hindered

88 Our hotel chain is _____ across the country for its quality service.

- A renowned
- B redeemed
- C remarkable
- D refined

89 A _____ is inserted to take blood, but it shouldn't hurt.

- A stake
- B needle
- C barrel
- D tube

90 Some _____ groups became violent during the protests.

- A fanatic
- B extremist
- C earnest
- D ardent

91 The orchestra will play a _____ by a new composer tonight.

- A dissertation
- B transmission
- C distribution
- D composition

92 People who _____ their work often become highly successful.

- A bury themselves in
- B make allowances for
- C have a soft spot for
- D owe their existence to

93 Drivers can be _____ by the headlights of oncoming traffic at night.

- A crushed
- B dazzled
- C constrained
- D dimmed

94 This semester's papers _____ the final grade for this course.

- A count with
- B count on
- C count up
- D count towards

95 At the end of summer, the swimming pool is _____ and cleaned.

- A flattened
- B curbed
- C expired
- D drained

96 Walking daily can certainly increase _____ for the majority of people.

- A longevity
- B persistence
- C expansion
- D durability

97 The shopping mall plans _____ some serious opposition from local stores.

- A ran up against
- B stuck up for
- C came down to
- D talked out of

98 Mr Daniel Davies is the newest _____ to the board of directors.

- A delegation
- B appointment
- C commission
- D fulfilment

99 It is far better to choose a perfume with a _____ fragrance rather than something overwhelming.

- A dull
- B pale
- C fragile
- D subtle

100 We decided to take a day trip to the beach _____.

- A every so often
- B on impulse
- C within limits
- D a fair amount

101 Alan was typing _____ in his office all day trying to meet his deadline.

- A almost
- B around
- C away
- D afar

102 Michael leant too hard on the tree branch and it _____.

- A unwound
- B rocked
- C snapped
- D clicked

This passage is about waste disposal.

Disposing of waste is one of society's greatest challenges. From plastic food packaging to chemicals used in manufacturing to the vast quantities of electronic waste cluttering up our homes, working out what to do with things we no longer want is often seen as the curse of modern living. It is estimated that, globally, people generate 350 million tonnes of plastic alone per year – double what it was at the turn of the century.

An even more depressing statistic is the amount of this plastic waste that is recycled, a figure that currently stands at a mere 9%, meaning vast quantities of plastic waste are still being sent to landfill. In addition, the latest reports about waste being dumped into seas and rivers make for grim reading to say the least.

Looking on the bright side though, new processes and approaches are gaining ground. In terms of recycling, there are plenty of start-ups throwing technological solutions at the problem (with some measure of success). New robots are powered by software programs that are far better than older recycling plants at sorting materials accurately and in much larger quantities. **They** are a welcome innovation in an industry that has notoriously tight margins. There are so many glues, inks and other ingredients that are difficult to dispose of that it's no wonder that so many recycling companies go out of business.

Of course, there are a couple of glaringly obvious approaches to disposing of waste. Firstly, companies should change the raw materials they use for biodegradable materials and adjust their processes to produce less waste wherever possible. Secondly, consumers could increase their awareness of the issue and act accordingly

103 What is the main purpose of the passage?
- A to educate people about how to recycle more
- B to explore new approaches to waste management
- C to predict the best solutions to waste disposal
- D to explain how waste pollutes the environment

104 What is the author's view of recent accounts about waste?
- A they are overly concerned with statistics
- B they don't contain sufficient details
- C people don't read enough of them
- D they contain disturbing information

105 In the fourth sentence of paragraph 3, what does **they** refer to?
- A materials
- B software programs
- C robots
- D recycling plants

106 What does the passage say about recycling businesses?
- A they are not particularly lucrative
- B they are at the forefront of innovation
- C they embrace complex challenges
- D they do not have a promising future

107 What advice does the passage give to companies?
- A they should listen to feedback from their customers
- B they don't need to make complicated changes
- C they must implement changes immediately
- D they shouldn't be reluctant to make changes

by choosing products with minimal waste, or by consuming less in the first place. Although it can be time consuming on an individual level, there is plenty that diligent, forward-thinking citizens can do, so it's worth taking action. Many a large organization has had to make a U-turn on waste-disposal policies following consumer complaints, or, more likely, as a reaction to a drop in sales when consumers decide to take their business elsewhere.

108 What is the author's point in the final paragraph?

  A consumers can effect change more than they think

  B companies will change their policies if enough people complain

  C companies want to keep up with purchasing trends

  D consumers have a bad attitude towards reducing waste

| 103 | A | B | C | D | | 104 | A | B | C | D | | 105 | A | B | C | D | | 106 | A | B | C | D |
| 107 | A | B | C | D | | 108 | A | B | C | D |

This passage is about toys.

It is always difficult to imagine everyday life in ancient societies, but one subject that has long puzzled archaeologists and historians is the everyday life of children and to what extent it differs from that of children today. There is far less documented about the lives of children in the ancient civilisations such as the Greeks, Romans or Aztecs compared to those of adults. This means that when archaeologists find artefacts that they suspect might be toys, they run into all sorts of difficulties trying to confirm whether their hunches are accurate or simply wild guesses.

For one thing, where an object is found, or its 'context' as archaeologists refer to it, is not always as useful as might be expected. For example, a doll found in a child's tomb may have had a ceremonial function rather than being a plaything. Similarly, children may have played with pots and pans in ancient civilisations in much the same way as they do in modern kitchens, yet finding kitchen utensils in a context connected with children does not count as evidence of this.

The situation is further compounded by the lack of attention from academics as it appears that studying the lives of ancient children has been far down the list of priorities of **many**. Nowadays, however, interest is growing, and various myths and assumptions are being dispelled. One of these is that, in the civilizations of the past, society had little interest in the lives of children; they rarely played and therefore did not require toys. However, written accounts exist of toys being given as gifts as well as descriptions of the toys that adults and their children played with. Another reliable source of evidence is through illustrations rather than texts. Vases, tombstones and other objects provide a rich source of images depicting children playing with toys, although, again, archaeologists advise caution when interpreting these images.

109 What is the main purpose of the passage?
- A to explain the difficulties of interpreting evidence
- B to give an overview of archaeological techniques
- C to show how research problems are being overcome
- D to outline types of childhood objects uncovered on digs

110 Why is the archaeology of toys different from other areas of archaeology?
- A there are very few physical examples of ancient toys
- B there is a lack of recorded information concerning ancient toys
- C there is no easy way to identify the function of the objects found
- D most images and documents are misleading on the subject

111 What does the passage say about context?
- A it is redundant
- B it is deceptive
- C it is indispensable
- D it is versatile

112 In the first sentence of paragraph 3, what does the word **many** refer to?
- A lives
- B priorities
- C academics
- D children

113 What is a more recent discovery concerning ancient toys?
- A they usually had more than one function
- B some were played with by all ages
- C most children rarely used their toys
- D they originally contained images

It is easy to imagine that an object looks similar to a modern toy when in all likelihood it would have had a completely different purpose in the ancient world, perhaps one more practical or related to religious practices.

Today's archaeologists have **a trick up their sleeves** that, until recently, has been unavailable: technology. Whereas, in the past, assessments of whether objects were for children meant focusing on how well they had been crafted or interpreting the context of the site where they were found, today's analytical methods are much more scientific and can include, among other techniques, fingerprint analysis. In this way, the mysteries of ancient toys are gradually being uncovered.

114 In the first sentence of paragraph 4, what word could best replace **a trick up their sleeve**?

   A   an advantage
   B   an approach
   C   an effort
   D   an attempt

| 109 | A | B | C | D |
| 113 | A | B | C | D |

| 110 | A | B | C | D |
| 114 | A | B | C | D |

| 111 | A | B | C | D |

| 112 | A | B | C | D |

This passage is about elite sports.

The pressure that elite sports players are under is almost impossible for us mere mortals to grasp. The fear of hitting a home run, running the hundred meters or taking a penalty shot in front of a crowd of thousands as the cacophonous noise rises up through a stadium is unthinkable for anyone not trained to manage **it**. And yet, elite sports players willingly put themselves in the spotlight to perform under this kind of pressure week in week out.

To ensure that this pressure does not become overwhelming, a variety of techniques are employed by elite sports people. These days psychology is at the forefront of this preparation. It is vital that athletes are able to stay focussed, practice techniques and hone their skills over long periods of time, and, most significantly, bounce back from defeats. Having strength, pace and ability is not enough for an athlete to reach the top and stay there. Elite sports players need a positive mindset as well as resilience when they face losses or absences due to injury.

Many elite sports players stress the importance of focusing on goal setting and approaching their sport with a personal desire to improve rather than **succumbing** to pressures from outside, be they from family or society. They take each game as it comes and use defeats as opportunities to learn and improve. The enjoyment that they get from practicing over and over in order to improve is what sets them apart from others, and this contributes to their elite status. They are not concerned with the judgement that comes from the media or fans because they understand how easy it is to let negative talk undermine their confidence.

However, just as physical skills require commitment over time, mental toughness cannot be achieved overnight either. It too

115 What is the main purpose of the passage?
   A to show how psychologists study elite sports players
   B to explain how elite sports players practice
   C to outline how physical factors impact upon success
   D to describe how elite sports players manage their mental health

116 In the second sentence of paragraph 1, what does **it** refer to?
   A fear
   B noise
   C shot
   D crowd

117 What does the author say elite sports players need?
   A constructive criticism from coaches
   B the desire to win at any cost
   C the ability to overcome setbacks
   D better stamina than everyone else

118 In the first sentence of paragraph 3, what word could best replace **succumb**?
   A resign
   B surrender
   C abandon
   D withdraw

119 How do elite sports players react to criticism?
   A they are able to put it aside
   B they react badly to it
   C they become less confident
   D they use it to set goals

requires setting measurable goals. Coaches and psychologists can play an important role in this by developing personalized plans that work towards creating the right attitudes for athletes. Having complementary physical and mental training regimes can go a long way towards ensuring that elite sports players keep the pressure they face in perspective.

120 What point does the author make about training elite sports players?

- **A** it takes longer to train the mind than the body
- **B** players need to change their attitudes to training
- **C** programs should address the body and mind equally
- **D** coaches should implement specific techniques

Reading ECPE
Test 8

51 Sally was annoyed because the meeting _____ in an hour and she was stuck in traffic.

A was just starting
B is due to start
C had been due to start
D was due to start

52 When witnesses come to the police station, the reception staff _____ in an interview room until an officer becomes available.

A have them sitting
B having them to sit
C have them to be sitting
D have them sit

53 My boss speaks so quietly I don't understand a word he says, and _____.

A neither do anyone
B nor does anyone else
C not any others do
D anyone else doesn't

54 We would be grateful if customers would be _____ check that they have all their belongings before leaving.

A as kind to
B so kind as to
C so kind to
D as so kind to

55 The Dean _____ dedicated to making this college the most successful it can possibly be.

A is to be only but
B is nothing if not
C is nothing except
D it's only to be

56 _____ my music teacher in high school, I'd never have decided to try out for this talent show.

A If it weren't for
B Were it not
C If it hadn't for
D It wasn't for

57 After the department store opened, many smaller stores _____ because they lost so much custom.

A resigned and closed themselves
B resigned themselves to closing
C had to resign to close
D were to resign and close

58 The Eagles are playing so badly this season that _____ stay in the league.

A they will bound not to
B they are not bounded to
C they're bound not to
D they won't be bound to

51	A	B	C	D		52	A	B	C	D		53	A	B	C	D		54	A	B	C	D
55	A	B	C	D		56	A	B	C	D		57	A	B	C	D		58	A	B	C	D

59 _____ almost an hour to speak to a manager, but not one person has come to ask if I'm oaky.

- **A** I have been waiting not only
- **B** Not only I have been waiting
- **C** I am waiting not only
- **D** Not only have I been waiting

60 _____, Chris couldn't seem to bake a birthday cake that looked really impressive.

- **A** Although he might try
- **B** He might have tried
- **C** Try as he might
- **D** As he might try

61 If you're thinking of taking the train downtown, you _____ leave now as they are always delayed.

- **A** might be well to
- **B** may as well
- **C** may as well to
- **D** might be well

62 _____ relocate to Miami next year, I'd have to look for another job.

- **A** Whether the company will
- **B** If the company could
- **C** Had the company to
- **D** Were the company to

63 The college _____ the excellent teaching staff.

- **A** attributes its success to
- **B** attributes success at
- **C** successful attribute is
- **D** is a successful attribute of

64 This year the environment was virtually ignored by the mayor, who allocated _____ funding to green projects.

- **A** less or nothing
- **B** little or no
- **C** low or small
- **D** few or none

65 Now he's been caught for speeding, his future as a cab driver will be _____ company.

- **A** in the hands of his
- **B** with the hand of the
- **C** from the hands of the
- **D** at the hand of his

66 Kate isn't in the office today, and, _____, I don't think I've seen her all week.

- **A** as to think about it
- **B** come to think of it
- **C** to come thinking of it
- **D** for thinking about it

Reading ECPE

This passage is about hurricanes.

Tropical storms called hurricanes are common occurrences along the shores of the USA from early summer to November. Notable for their high winds and **67)**_____ rain, as well as the damage they cause to coastline infrastructure, their **68)**_____ effects can extend further inland than people expect.

The National Hurricane Center monitors hurricanes and **69)**_____ one is identified as likely to **70)**_____ local communities, their role is to **71)**_____ warnings and advice. When a storm **72)**_____ on the horizon, the Center will usually suggest that people secure any loose tools or gardening equipment. This is a **73)**_____ to prevent further property damage rather than an attempt to protect personal possessions. Once the storm hits land, citizens are advised not to **74)**_____ at all in order to prevent unnecessary accidents at a time when the emergency services will be under severe pressure.

Florida and Texas are **75)**_____ these storms more often than other states, in part due to the ocean temperature on the east coast and the Gulf of Mexico. The gulf stream maintains the water temperature above 80 degrees, which allows hurricanes to form. On the Pacific coast, however, the water is far too cold to **76)**_____ them.

67	A	turbulent	C	torrential
	B	scattered	D	mighty

68	A	intolerable	C	formidable
	B	explosive	D	devastating

69	A	whenever	C	reportedly
	B	swiftly	D	whereby

70	A	assault	C	disturb
	B	weaken	D	threaten

71	A	emit	C	issue
	B	utter	D	allege

72	A	looms	C	erupts
	B	depicts	D	breaks

73	A	shrewd principle	C	routine motion
	B	pragmatic measure	D	subtle move

74	A	set sail	C	carry weight
	B	venture outside	D	pace around

75	A	on the brink of	C	along the lines of
	B	in conjunction with	D	at the mercy of

76	A	uphold	C	sustain
	B	conceive	D	yield

Part 2 | Multiple-choice Cloze | Test 8

This passage is about yoga.

In the USA, almost a quarter of large businesses provide some kind of yoga or meditation opportunities to their workforce. While this seems a significant amount, there are strong arguments for employers to adopt this **77)**_____ and rid themselves of any **78)**_____ ideas around promoting well-being in the workplace.

In offices across the country, working time is **79)**_____ lost to **80)**_____ back pain, largely due to employees sitting at desks for large periods of time, and this has a **81)**_____ on overall productivity. Just adding in short classes comprising a gentle warm-up, some key spinal stretches and posture exercises, as well as some relaxation techniques, can effectively **82)**_____ these issues.

After following this routine for eight weeks, one organization saw a huge reduction in general employee back pain, and twenty times less **83)**_____ caused by back pain. The productivity of the workforce also increased. Those who improved most significantly were employees who **84)**_____ their workplace yoga routines with further workouts at home.

Therefore, **85)**_____ that the growing interest in yoga and meditation in the workplace can **86)**_____ for both employers and employees.

77	A	behind the scenes	C	across the board
	B	on the face of it	D	out of the ordinary

78	A	cynical	C	lenient
	B	assertive	D	disruptive

79	A	consistently	C	realistically
	B	hopelessly	D	technically

80	A	irritable	C	infectious
	B	rigid	D	chronic

81	A	sore point	C	profound effect
	B	vain attempt	D	sharp turn

82	A	drain	C	narrow
	B	combat	D	refrain

83	A	health absence	C	sick leave
	B	medical diagnosis	D	feeling faint

84	A	revived	C	intensified
	B	overlapped	D	supplemented

85	A	it serves a purpose	C	it sets standards
	B	it stands to reason	D	it speaks for itself

86	A	reap rewards	C	wield influence
	B	follow suit	D	loom large

77	A	B	C	D		78	A	B	C	D		79	A	B	C	D		80	A	B	C	D
81	A	B	C	D		82	A	B	C	D		83	A	B	C	D		84	A	B	C	D
85	A	B	C	D		86	A	B	C	D												

87 The fans enthusiastically _____ their team for the entire match.

- **A** called for
- **B** cheered on
- **C** cried out
- **D** cracked up

88 A Branston alarm is the most effective way of deterring _____ from houses.

- **A** interrupters
- **B** infiltrators
- **C** intruders
- **D** interferers

89 She _____ her bag tightly as she walked through the crowds in the city.

- **A** clutched
- **B** clashed
- **C** confined
- **D** conditioned

90 The best _____ on this ship are on the top deck.

- **A** cubicles
- **B** cabins
- **C** chambers
- **D** cells

91 If they want to agree a deal, one of the parties needs to make some _____.

- **A** concessions
- **B** revelations
- **C** permissions
- **D** expositions

92 The _____ mornings in the fall are what make Boston such a special city.

- **A** crumbly
- **B** crude
- **C** crusty
- **D** crisp

93 Most workmen include a _____ of costs for each job.

- **A** diagnosis
- **B** stopgap
- **C** auxiliary
- **D** breakdown

94 The situation was so funny that Sonia could hardly _____.

- **A** put her foot in it
- **B** laugh her head off
- **C** keep a straight face
- **D** pull a muscle

95 The place was completely _____ so they decided to go somewhere more exciting.

   A asleep
   B dead
   C spent
   D inert

96 Sophie just about managed to _____ all her belongings into the trunk of her car.

   A anchor
   B patch
   C signal
   D jam

97 During fall we _____ as much wood as possible for the winter.

   A store up
   B work out
   C provide for
   D look ahead

98 The neighbors _____ in having loud parties at the weekends.

   A consent
   B initiate
   C persist
   D disclose

99 City Hall is _____ pushing forward with the plans, despite the opposition.

   A superficially
   B vaguely
   C relentlessly
   D strategically

100 I wish I hadn't _____ my friends' argument.

   A had a weakness for
   B gotten caught up in
   C been in tune with
   D put my finger on

101 Making eye _____ with an audience is a great way to engage them.

   A contact
   B touch
   C strike
   D network

102 Fewer species will _____ the rainforest if climate change continues.

   A inhabit
   B house
   C seize
   D prosper

This passage is about copycatting.

It seems common sense that, after all the time, money and effort spent on developing a brand or product, a company wouldn't want a competitor to just come along and make a copycat version, and it probably comes as no surprise to the seasoned businessperson that this happens almost constantly in the world of commerce. However, while companies are aware of this and often guard against it, the case of such copycat products is not as clear cut as it might seem.

Of course, there are a number of examples of leading original brand manufacturers going to the expense of taking legal action against other companies that have produced products that strike more than a passing similarity to their original versions. Likenesses could be in a variety of ways, including similarities in the coloring, lettering and placement of information on the products' packaging. In fact, some household-name grocery stores have clashed numerous times with big brands when the store's own-brand products have been accused of overstepping the mark, similarity-wise. It's easy to see why because, after years building a good name, some major brands are rightly sensitive about a newcomer riding the coat tails of this success.

But this form of 'copycatting' isn't necessarily the one-way street it seems at first. To begin with, there are many major brands that, for one reason or another, don't pursue this kind of activity through the courts. Perhaps because legal loopholes in how others have copied mean they have slim chance of success, but also this can be because they just don't see the merit in it, even realizing that sometimes there are some surprising perks of this kind of copying. For one, copycat products inadvertently highlight the major brand as the leader in the market. After all, why would you want to copy a **nonstarter**? This, therefore, becomes a form of free advertising for the main brand as their original design becomes more widespread, reminding consumers of the market-leading original product.

A final, interesting element to this activity is that perhaps the copycat, in at least some

103 What is the main purpose of the passage?
  A to explain how some companies copy products
  B to detail why copying products is illegal
  C to outline the financial benefits of copying products
  D to argue that copying products isn't always bad

104 Why do some companies sue others that copy their brand?
  A because the major brand has its profit margin lowered
  B because the copied brand is benefitting unjustly from others' work
  C because the copied brand is deliberately misleading the customer
  D because it negatively affects the major brand's reputation

105 According to the passage, why is legal action not advisable?
  A the odds of a triumph are low
  B the procedure is too lengthy
  C the system is overly complex
  D the costs of a trial are excessive

106 In paragraph 3, sentence 5, which word could best replace **nonstarter**?
  A farce
  B deficiency
  C flop
  D tragedy

107 How can copycatting benefit the original brand manufacturers?
  A it highlights their quality standards
  B it provides extra publicity
  C it attracts more customers
  D it improves their products

cases, isn't the competition that it at first seems. There are many marketing theorists who think that there is more to some stores' own brands than meets the eye, and that it's likely, although never strictly admitted, that in some cases the companies behind the major labels are producing the home-brand products too. While this may seem a strange concept, on further inspection it's a win-win for all concerned to some extent, even though sales of the original product may be affected: the manufacturer gets more business and can buy ingredients in larger quantities, therefore at lower manufacturing costs, and the store makes money from its own brand. However, it's the wider public that reaps the serious rewards, with a greater choice and cheaper (and often no less inferior) product offering.

108 Who benefits the most from large brands making stores' own-brand products?

- **A** the consumer
- **B** the grocery store
- **C** the sales teams
- **D** the manufacturer

This passage is about suburbs.

Suburbs are the areas around cities that comprise residential dwellings. When most people think of suburbs, what comes to mind is rows of spruce houses with picket fences, and vehicles parked outside ready for the daily commute. They don't necessarily conjure up the idea of life in the fast lane, but in 1950s America, they changed the landscape, not just geographically, but socially and economically.

Before the mid-1900s, there were huge numbers of citizens living in cramped, overcrowded conditions throughout cities in the United States. The accommodation was ill-equipped to deal with the sheer growth of city living, with many families sharing small apartments with others. However, all this changed with the introduction of nationwide programs to give government-**backed** loans to people who wanted to buy their own houses. This saw property developers grab land near the cities and develop whole swathes of residential communities or suburban areas with cheap, mass-made housing. In some ways this created the seeds of the concept known as the 'American Dream'. It gave hope to many that they could afford their own homes, their own gardens and a better way of life.

Quality of life for many of those moving to these new areas rose significantly, but the effects were far wider than this. The creation of these suburbs at such a breakneck speed dramatically stimulated growth in the USA. Streetcar lines and railroads were constructed, and the sale of automobiles rose dramatically as these new homeowners looked for ways to travel on their daily commute.

Additionally, as wages increased, goods became cheaper thanks to mass production. The US also saw a huge rise in consumption, as new proprietors looked for items to complete their homes, and shopping malls sprung up all over the USA. Credit started to be introduced at this time, along with instalment repayment plans so consumers could 'buy now', instead of save for later.

Nowadays the view of suburbs is perhaps more mixed than it used to be. Architecturally

109 What is the main purpose of the passage?
- A to highlight why suburbs are a unique feature of the USA
- B to explain the causes and effects of suburb growth in the USA
- C to outline the advantages and disadvantages of USA suburbs
- D to describe the attraction of living in the suburbs

110 How does the writer describe the reputation of suburbs in paragraph 1?
- A deceptive
- B bustling
- C mundane
- D universal

111 In paragraph 2, sentence 3, which word could best replace **backed**?
- A guaranteed
- B consolidated
- C distributed
- D influenced

112 What was one effect of the growth of suburbs?
- A building regulations
- B inflated earnings
- C community investment
- D infrastructure expansion

113 In paragraph 5, sentence 2, which phrase could best replace **in no uncertain terms**?
- A in all honesty
- B to say the least
- C at any rate
- D without a doubt

speaking, they are often accused of being a monotonous blot on the landscape, but, **in no uncertain terms**, they revolutionized the fortunes of America, and arguably made it into the country it is today.

114 What is the writer's overall opinion of suburbs in the USA?

- **A** they were more appealing in the past than now
- **B** they were fundamental in the growth of the country
- **C** they have made the countryside look increasingly dull
- **D** they provided opportunities for people to succeed in life

109	A	B	C	D
113	A	B	C	D

110	A	B	C	D
114	A	B	C	D

111	A	B	C	D

112	A	B	C	D

This passage is about Morse Code.

Most people around the world know something about Morse Code, even if they haven't heard the name before. For example, the 'SOS' signal, known worldwide as a signal of distress, is actually from Morse Code, whether written in dots or dashes, or letters. It may seem like a rather basic form of communication, but it has made a large difference in people's lives, and still continues to do so today, despite being overtaken in many ways by modern forms of communications technology.

In the past, emergency communication over any distance was virtually impossible. Rudimentary techniques were used to get messages across lands and seas, like smoke signals, flag waving or drumbeats, but these could only reach so far. This all changed with the invention of telegraph wires and Morse Code, and later the development of wireless telegraph systems at the end of the 19th Century. These advancements meant that people could send messages to each other in a more practical fashion, and over vastly longer distances.

One famous example of this has to be the sinking of *The Titanic* in 1912, when its Morse Code distress signals were picked up by cruise liner *The Carpathia*, which came to the rescue of around 700 survivors of the disaster. There are hundreds of other, **albeit** lesser known, examples of Morse Code delivering people from an untimely demise, especially, but not exclusively, at sea.

The reason for its popularity and effectiveness almost certainly lies in its simplicity. By utilizing a series of dots and dashes, people can use it when they can't use their voice, simply by flashing lights, knocking or blinking. It's not a system suited for long stretches of texts, and you wouldn't want to write a novel on it, but it communicates an essential message relatively easily: it's simply on or off, long or short.

However, communications have moved on, and Morse Code isn't as widely used as it once was. After all, nowadays anyone can pick up the phone, use the internet and communicate in a variety of fast and easy ways. This doesn't

115 What is the main purpose of the passage?
- A to explain how Morse Code works
- B to outline the continued relevance of Morse Code
- C to describe the development of Morse Code
- D to compare Morse Code to other communication methods

116 What does the passage imply about Morse Code and travelling at sea?
- A it improved safety
- B it became faster
- C it changed ship design
- D it brought loved ones closer

117 In paragraph 3, sentence 2 what word can replace **albeit**?
- A provided
- B besides
- C whereby
- D although

118 What is the key benefit of Morse Code?
- A its fame
- B its flexibility
- C its clarity
- D its speed

119 What does the text say about the recent change in use of Morse Code?
- A it was an unintended development
- B it was driven by the internet
- C it was adapted to cater for a specific group
- D it stopped Morse Code from dying out

mean that Morse Code is in obsolescence though. In fact, it has found a use that was a far cry from its original goal. Recently, due to the varied ways in which it can be transmitted, Morse Code has been the key to unlocking the door to the outside world for people who can't verbally communicate due to a medical condition or disability. So much so, that Google has added Morse Code to their Gboard to aid these kinds of communications. Additionally, there is no doubt that knowing at least the basic 'SOS' signal could still get you out of the most desperate of situations when you least expect it!

120 Who is Morse Code useful for today?

    A mainly only people with illnesses

    B everyone, to a varying extent

    C those without modern technology

    D people who work in dangerous situations

115	A	B	C	D
119	A	B	C	D

116	A	B	C	D
120	A	B	C	D

| 117 | A | B | C | D |

| 118 | A | B | C | D |

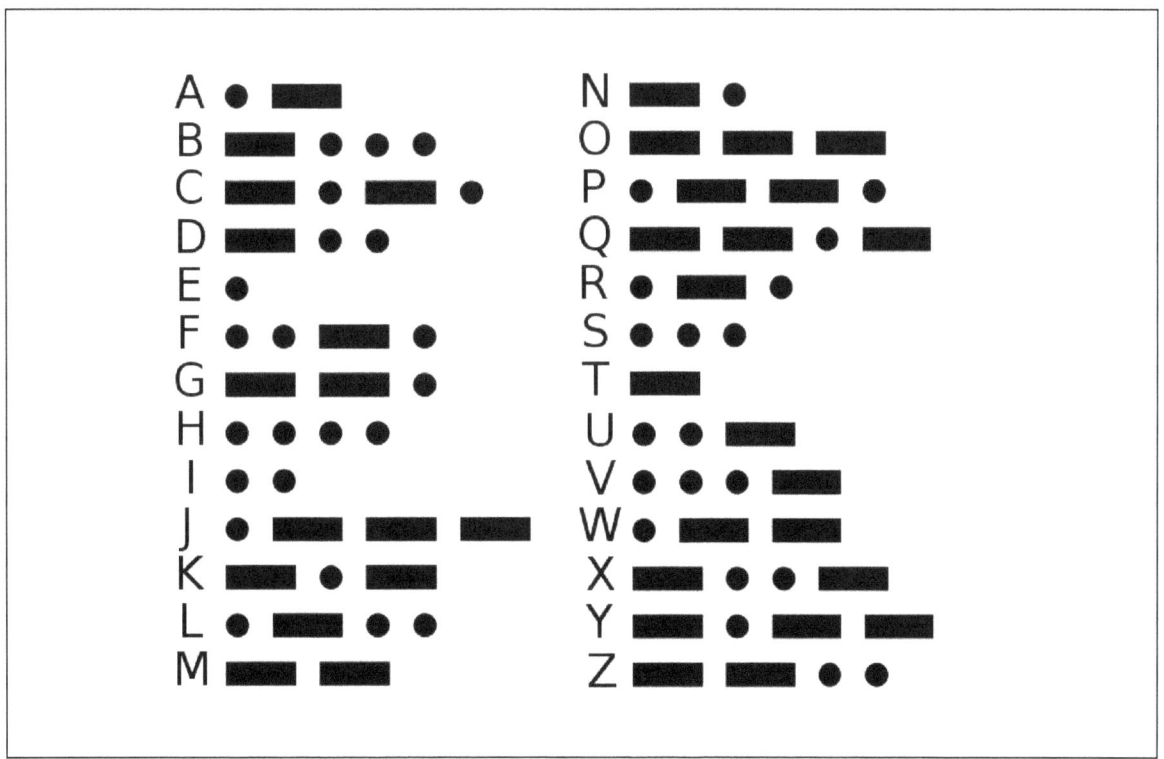

Answers

Answers | Test 1

#	Ans	#	Ans	#	Ans	#	Ans
51	B	69	D	86	D	103	B
52	A	70	D	87	D	104	B
53	C	71	C	88	A	105	B
54	B	72	B	89	D	106	D
55	D	73	C	90	C	107	A
56	D	74	A	91	A	108	C
57	B	75	D	92	D	109	C
58	D	76	A	93	B	110	C
59	B	77	C	94	C	111	B
60	D	78	D	95	B	112	D
61	A	79	A	96	A	113	D
62	B	80	A	97	C	114	A
63	D	81	C	98	B	115	B
64	C	82	B	99	D	116	D
65	C	83	B	100	B	117	C
66	B	84	D	101	D	118	B
67	B	85	A	102	A	119	C
68	A					120	B

Answers | Test 2

#	Ans	#	Ans	#	Ans	#	Ans
51	D	69	B	86	D	103	B
52	C	70	D	87	B	104	C
53	A	71	A	88	A	105	D
54	A	72	C	89	A	106	D
55	C	73	A	90	D	107	B
56	D	74	B	91	A	108	A
57	C	75	C	92	B	109	C
58	B	76	D	93	B	110	D
59	B	77	A	94	D	111	C
60	B	78	D	95	D	112	A
61	D	79	B	96	B	113	B
62	C	80	D	97	D	114	A
63	A	81	C	98	A	115	D
64	A	82	A	99	C	116	D
65	B	83	B	100	C	117	B
66	C	84	C	101	A	118	B
67	C	85	C	102	B	119	B
68	A					120	B

Answers | Test 3

#	Ans	#	Ans	#	Ans	#	Ans
51	B	69	B	86	C	103	A
52	C	70	B	87	A	104	B
53	C	71	D	88	D	105	A
54	A	72	D	89	D	106	B
55	C	73	C	90	A	107	C
56	B	74	C	91	B	108	D
57	D	75	B	92	D	109	D
58	A	76	A	93	D	110	D
59	B	77	B	94	B	111	A
60	D	78	A	95	C	112	C
61	D	79	C	96	D	113	C
62	D	80	A	97	C	114	B
63	C	81	D	98	A	115	C
64	B	82	C	99	C	116	B
65	B	83	D	100	A	117	A
66	C	84	B	101	A	118	D
67	A	85	A	102	B	119	A
68	D					120	B

Answers | Test 4

#	Ans	#	Ans	#	Ans	#	Ans
51	C	69	B	86	D	103	B
52	C	70	D	87	C	104	D
53	B	71	A	88	B	105	D
54	D	72	C	89	A	106	A
55	A	73	A	90	C	107	C
56	B	74	B	91	D	108	A
57	D	75	C	92	D	109	A
58	D	76	D	93	B	110	B
59	C	77	B	94	B	111	C
60	C	78	D	95	A	112	D
61	D	79	C	96	A	113	D
62	A	80	D	97	C	114	C
63	A	81	B	98	C	115	B
64	B	82	A	99	B	116	D
65	A	83	A	100	A	117	D
66	C	84	C	101	B	118	A
67	D	85	D	102	D	119	B
68	C					120	B

Answers | Test 5

#	Ans	#	Ans	#	Ans	#	Ans
51	A	69	A	86	A	103	B
52	A	70	D	87	C	104	D
53	D	71	A	88	A	105	D
54	D	72	C	89	A	106	A
55	B	73	B	90	B	107	B
56	C	74	C	91	A	108	C
57	C	75	D	92	C	109	B
58	A	76	A	93	A	110	A
59	C	77	C	94	A	111	C
60	B	78	A	95	D	112	B
61	A	79	B	96	D	113	D
62	C	80	A	97	C	114	D
63	C	81	D	98	A	115	C
64	B	82	C	99	B	116	A
65	C	83	D	100	C	117	D
66	A	84	B	101	B	118	B
67	B	85	C	102	C	119	D
68	B					120	D

Answers | Test 6

#	Ans	#	Ans	#	Ans	#	Ans
51	B	69	D	86	D	103	C
52	B	70	D	87	A	104	B
53	D	71	A	88	D	105	A
54	B	72	D	89	A	106	D
55	C	73	A	90	C	107	D
56	C	74	A	91	C	108	B
57	A	75	C	92	B	109	B
58	D	76	B	93	B	110	C
59	A	77	C	94	A	111	D
60	D	78	A	95	B	112	C
61	A	79	B	96	D	113	D
62	C	80	B	97	D	114	B
63	B	81	D	98	A	115	C
64	C	82	C	99	D	116	D
65	A	83	A	100	B	117	B
66	C	84	A	101	B	118	A
67	C	85	C	102	B	119	D
68	B					120	B

Answers | Test 7

#	Ans	#	Ans	#	Ans	#	Ans
51	D	69	D	86	B	103	B
52	D	70	A	87	C	104	D
53	B	71	B	88	A	105	C
54	C	72	A	89	B	106	A
55	D	73	D	90	B	107	B
56	B	74	D	91	D	108	A
57	C	75	B	92	A	109	A
58	A	76	C	93	B	110	C
59	B	77	A	94	D	111	B
60	B	78	C	95	D	112	C
61	C	79	B	96	A	113	B
62	C	80	C	97	A	114	A
63	D	81	A	98	B	115	D
64	A	82	D	99	D	116	A
65	C	83	B	100	B	117	C
66	D	84	D	101	C	118	B
67	B	85	C	102	C	119	A
68	C					120	C

Answers | Test 8

#	Ans	#	Ans	#	Ans	#	Ans
51	D	69	A	86	A	103	D
52	D	70	D	87	B	104	B
53	B	71	C	88	C	105	D
54	B	72	A	89	A	106	C
55	B	73	B	90	B	107	B
56	A	74	B	91	A	108	A
57	B	75	D	92	D	109	B
58	C	76	C	93	D	110	C
59	D	77	C	94	C	111	A
60	C	78	A	95	B	112	D
61	B	79	A	96	D	113	D
62	D	80	D	97	A	114	B
63	A	81	C	98	C	115	B
64	B	82	B	99	C	116	A
65	A	83	C	100	B	117	D
66	B	84	D	101	A	118	B
67	C	85	B	102	A	119	A
68	D					120	B

www.ingramcontent.com/pod-product-compliance
Lightning Source LLC
Chambersburg PA
CBHW042019090526
44590CB00029B/4333